A MOTHER'S GIFT TO A WAR-TORN NATION

Thomas J. Shattock

MINERVA PRESS

ATLANTA LONDON SYDNEY

A MOTHER'S GIFT TO A WAR-TORN NATION
Copyright © Thomas J. Shattock 1999

ISBN 0 75410 600 4

First Published 1999 by
MINERVA PRESS
315–317 Regent Street
London W1R 7YB

Printed in Great Britain for Minerva Press

A MOTHER'S GIFT TO A WAR-TORN NATION

I wish to take this opportunity to express my profound thanks to Pat Nutly and all my friends who over the years encouraged me to get my story published. This I could not have achieved had it not been for the sponsorship of my son Roy. Also for my daughter Maureen who has acted as my liaison during this project.

Foreword

During my declining years the Southend on Sea branch of the Royal Naval Association provides the ideal atmosphere to suit the requirements of six of us Second World War submariners and our wives. There at lunch time every Wednesday, we sit beneath the swinging lamps with our feet awash in briny foam. Wide-eyed and all agog our wives have to suffer the mental torture of being depth-charged.

During one of these yarn-spinning sessions, my wife discovered that all my pals had reached the dizzy heights of either petty officer or chief petty officer. Somewhat puzzled she asked, 'Why were all your pals promoted and not you?' She then added, 'You must have been a sod in the Navy.'

So being taunted by those inspiring accolades I launch this true story of the most exciting years of my life – my twelve years in the Royal Navy. For you to judge is my full confession and the revelation of my exploits during those bygone years.

Was I a sod in the Navy or a mother's gift to a war-torn nation?

Submarine Triad's *Crew*
The author is the second rating on the left
From the Radio Times Hulton Picture Library

'HMS/m Thrasher' *by John Pettitt*
Courtesy of the Royal Navy Submarine Museum, Gosport

Glossary

asdic	Detection apparatus also known as ping bosum
ERA	Engine room artificer
gash	Culinary waste (in those days kept in buckets for easy disposal over the side)
killick	The badge of office worn on leading hands left arm, (a small anchor) hence the name, killick
number elevens	Rifle drill or fatigue duties (to deprive offenders of their leisure hours)
Outside ERA	Responsible for all machinery outside the engine room

Chapter One
A Mother's Gift

During the Thirties the dole queues had been steadily increasing, and by February 1937 when I reached my nineteenth birthday, I too found myself unemployed. With no prospect of getting a job I decided to join the Royal Navy. After preliminary enquiries I was summoned to Admiralty House, Whitehall, London. There I was passed medically fit but to my dismay I was almost rejected due to my poor education. My lessons during my last year at school had been constantly interrupted because of the appalling record which I acquired for playing truant. I assumed that the experience that I had accumulated in my chequered working life would outweigh the dull, theoretical knowledge acquired by scholarly types who had wormed their way through the classroom textbooks. Such was my reasoning in those hard times which we endured in the Depression of the Thirties. However, in their infinite wisdom, their Lordships decided to accept me into the Royal Navy as a Stoker Second Class, thus committing me to serve twelve years of the most adventurous time of my life.

I was one of forty applicants who had successfully applied for training in Chatham where we were divided into two groups for discipline training. The first of these groups was destined to become seamen and the other, stokers. The group to which I was assigned was the latter which came to be known as 129 class and we were to be instructed by Leading Seaman Payne who immediately introduced himself as 'Whacker'. He then explained that the sense of pain was known to the Navy as a 'whacker'. There can be little doubt that this terminology derived from his earlier days when he served as a boy sailor. In those days a defaulting lad would be given the cane, hence, a 'whacker'. During my early days Whacker amused the squad by telling them that he had made a marvellous discovery.

'I have found a sailor with two left feet,' he said, and being graced with cockney humour and a boyish manner he turned to me and dubbed me with the name 'Stupid'. For the duration of my square bashing I had no option but to accept this title and outwardly rejoiced in it, after all there had to be a stooge in every squad. It was just my misfortune to have joined up with a bunch of ex-territorial and other trainees who had benefited from previous drill instructions from one source or another.

My inability to comply with the various commands on the parade ground more than once gave the instructor real cause to have the whole class pounding up and down Constitution Hill with rifles at the slope. This punishment would sometimes continue for an hour or more, after which time our white canvas duck suits would be soaked with perspiration and our left shoulders rubbed raw. No wonder my classmates wasted no time addressing me by my new tag. As to my response to these taunts, outwardly I joined in the fun, as it seemed to them it was like water off a duck's back, they couldn't hurt me. How wrong they were because inwardly I was very sensitive and began to doubt my own ability.

It was indeed a worrying time for me and it was not until years later that I realised the purpose of it all. It was just the Navy's way of building up strength of character, and it worked. I sought desperately to fight my way out of these situations but alas the method I chose led me into more trouble. On the parade ground I think I became Whacker's nightmare. From his point of view our class was the first that he had ever instructed so he had to make a success of it. A country boy from Norfolk who had recently joined the squad did little to improve Whacker's temper. With his wobbling gait I imagined him to be a skilful ploughman but definitely not suited to take part in the various manoeuvres on the parade ground. From time to time I would juggle my position in the ranks in order to get away from him but after a few manoeuvres, there he would appear again, right in front of me. His feet seemed to spread all over the place and invariably we would finish up on a collision course for which I would always take the blame.

Whacker would glare at me and bawl at the top of his voice, 'Look at him, he is a mother's gift to a war-torn nation.' Then to his annoyance I would respond with a giggle as if treating the whole thing as a joke.

While my apparent levity in these situations seemed to bring mirth to my classmates, Whacker would show no sign of enjoying the joke, he would instead be stamping up and down between the ranks doing his nut.

Towards the end of three months' rigorous training I became well established as the squad's clown. This had become a new role for me, and while the laughs were coming one a minute I was rejoicing in my new popularity among my classmates. For this reason I would often play to the gallery and this got me into even more trouble.

About this time they held the Chatham New Entries swimming competitions and I without telling my class-mates had entered for the 100 yards breaststroke. Although I thought that I had won the race I was disqualified to second place because on my last turn I did not touch the end of the bath with both hands. However late that evening it appeared that Whacker had got to hear about it because he came to the mess to congratulate me but not without giving me plenty of stick for not telling them so that they could have come along to give me a cheer. It seemed at last I had done something to please him.

Finally the day came for the passing out parade. It was a dismal morning and by ten o'clock the rain was pouring down in torrents so the gunnery officer decided to inspect us inside the drill shed. He was a well-known character who had only one eye which apparently sufficed for his exacting demands. As we marched to the covers of the drill shed I could see him standing in the distance ready to scrutinise our antics, and as we reached him we broke ranks to remove our oilskins. We were then ordered to form two ranks ready for inspection.

Whacker was about to march us towards him when he stopped dead in his tracks, then looking me straight in the eye he whispered, 'If you let me down you b— I will kill you.' This time I did not grin back at him.

For the next half hour he really put us through our paces and our response was immediate. With every drill carried out to perfection I could see that Whacker couldn't believe his eyes. There was not a single flaw in our performance.

With all drills now completed it was time for Whacker to report back to the gunnery officer and wait for his assessment. It soon became quite evident that Whacker had been well commended for his labours.

As he stood before us as proud as a peacock with his face beaming with delight, he uttered one word: 'Guardsmen.'

He then stalked up to me and said, 'As for you, you sod, all these past three months you have been pulling my pisser.'

He then told us how proud he was of each and every one of us and proceeded to march us back to the gunnery school to return our rifles. Soon we were all sitting in our mess back in the barrack room and after giving us a pep talk, he introduced us to Chief Stoker Cooper who was to be our engineering instructor for the next three months. Under his guidance Whacker told us that the rest of our training would be implemented within the bounds of the classroom. Then, after our class leader had presented him with a small gift from us all, he gave us a firm handshake and left us to continue on to the next stage of our adventure.

Chapter Two
All at Sea

The gentle manner in which Chief Stoker Cooper introduced himself was far removed from Whacker's barking
commands on the parade ground. In many ways, life in the
classroom was a lot easier, but for some strange reason I
began to miss our energetic stints in the open air, especially
during those hot sultry summer afternoons when I would
be sitting in the classroom half asleep trying to cope with
the ever-increasing flow of instructions about the workings
of boilers and a whole range of machinery in ships. Having
no mechanical knowledge whatsoever it all seemed very
foreign to me. Towards the end of August, having just
scraped through my final examination, I was drafted to the
light cruiser HMS *Arethusa*. This fine ship had just commissioned and was due to return to the Mediterranean Sea.
I was especially pleased when I saw the name of Harry
Carpenter just below mine. He was one of a dozen of my
classmates sent on the same draft. Like all Carpenters in the
Navy he was dubbed with the name tag 'Chippy'. My close
friendship with him started soon after we joined the Navy.
It began one Friday when our watch was due for a long
weekend. I had noticed that Chippy had made no attempt
to get changed into his shore-going clobber. Suspecting that
he had nowhere to go I invited him to spend a weekend
with me at my home in Southend. That was a beginning of
a shore-going partnership that was to continue for the next

two years.

A steam-easy approach to my duties is perhaps one of the few regrets I have. In those days my only ambition was to don a sailor's suit and enjoy as much time ashore as money and leave would permit. Mere details like learning my job in the boiler rooms I could only view as a secondary objective.

To fulfil my duties as a stoker second class I was assigned to keep auxiliary watches in No. 1 boiler room. The chief of the watch was a young acting PO who answered to the name of Farrel. He was a tall lean man with sunken cheeks and bulbous eyes. Smartly dressed in a tailor-made boiler suit he looked a promising candidate for rapid promotion. There was however, a fly in the ointment: me! I would prove very soon that I was going to be of little help towards his success in fulfilling such ambitions.

When I took my first steps on the footplates below, he formally introduced himself. He then proceeded to bombard me with a whole series of questions ranging from my town of origin, my former employment, sporting activities, had I been at sea before and what did I think of the Navy. Having provided him with the answers to these numerous questions it was up to him to form his own opinion about my future prospects.

As I made a quick survey of my new surroundings, it did not occur to me that I had taken a step along a path leading me into hidden traps and hazards which were to plague me for the next two years. It seemed to me that I had a natural ability to become involved in misdemeanours on the part of others. When anything went wrong I was never far away from the scene.

At this time I was about to take up my duties in the boiler room. This was after a previous tour in the company of PO Farrel, who explained to me the various functions of the main and auxiliary feed pumps, as well as the complicated maze of steam pipes, all of which contrive to supply the ship with the necessary power to control a man-of-war at sea. However this was my first watch below, the ship was in port and the only power that was needed was for auxiliary purposes, such as steam to drive electric generators for lighting, and hot water for general use.

In order to bring the boiler to life it was necessary to have the correct air pressure to ensure the complete combustion of the oil fuel, the latter being supplied to the boiler by means of a spray valve. When turned on the ejected spray was ignited by means of a fired torch which consisted of an iron poker with a nest of cotton waste tied to the end of it and after being dipped into a bucket of oil fuel and lit with a match, the flaming torch was placed into a port adjacent to the spray and with a turn on the control valve, the preheated high pressure fuel would be forced through the nozzle of the spray and ignite. Having reached the required steam pressure the stop valve would then be opened and the boiler would be in operation.

When entering my mess for the first time the senior leading stoker gave me instructions appertaining to the general routine in the mess. Then writing my name on the bottom of 'the cook of the mess' roster he told me to familiarise myself with the routine list. This meant that once a week for a period of twenty-four hours I and a designated partner would be responsible for collecting the meals from the ship's galley, washing up the crocks and scrubbing out the mess after breakfast. A few days later when my name appeared at the top of the list, I set off to find the whereabouts of the chef's domain. During my search I soon discovered that a second class stoker was regarded as fair game for a few smart alecks or clever dicks to exercise their warped minds in a spot of leg-pulling.

As I stepped on the upper-deck I found myself among a group of seasoned stokers, one of whom seemed most helpful. He was a funny little man who wore a jet-black beard with a sharp pointed moustache. He had a small but muscular body which seemed to move about in short sharp jerks. I used to imagine that he had escaped from a circus.

'Can you tell me where the galley is?' I asked.

'Just go through that door and ask sloshy if you can have the dinner for twenty-six mess,' he said.

'Sloshy?' I queried.

'Yes that's right. We never call them chefs aboard a ship,' he answered.

Being totally unsuspecting I went through to the galley and asked for the dinners. As Chef handed me two large dishes I acknowledged his helping hand as I thought a real seafarer should.

'Thanks Sloshy,' I said to him.

'Sloshy?' he screamed. 'Don't you know who I am?'

'No, sir,' came my timid reply.

I stood there shaking in my shoes as he thundered into my ears, 'I am the chief cook on this ship. Now get out of my galley.'

In a way I was able to take a philosophical view, it was at least one way of finding out who's who but from experience I couldn't recommend it.

Two weeks later while the ship was at anchor and only secondary use of power was required, I was on watch in No. 1 boiler room. From time to time it became necessary for me to shut off the spray valve and allow the steam pressure to drop back. Then, having dropped back ten pound per square inch or so, the whole procedure of flashing up would start again.

Such were the conditions on that particular Sunday when the whole fleet was at rest in the Grand Harbour at Malta. The quarterdeck was sheltered by an immaculate white canopy and the whole ship's company was assembled on the upper-deck garbed in their white suits. As for the scene down below, I had accidentally left the spray valve partly open thereby flooding the interior of the unlit boiler with the volatile heated oil fuel. It was about ten o'clock in the morning and the needle on the pressure gauge had dropped below the required pressure. I then decided to flash up again. As I applied the lighted torch to the spray, the boiler's response was immediate and may I add, so was the unsuspecting POs. With a thunderous flash the whole boiler seemed to leap forward thus blowing myself and the stoker PO before it and almost pinning us to the front of the boiler behind us. Totally lost for an explanation I looked into the terror-stricken face of Stoker PO Farrel and judging from his ashen cheeks one would have thought that he had spent the morning in the company of Count Dracula brandishing a flame thrower. Had there been a mirror in the boiler room it would have reflected a do-it-yourself Kojak minus the eyebrows and lollipop.

A flashback is not entirely unknown in the Royal Navy but this one had to be the daddy of them all, because both the situation and timing were unique. Imagine the flagship and showpiece of the Mediterranean Fleet, with all its officers and ratings adorned in white and smartly paraded on the upper-deck. The occasion was for Sunday divisions. In peacetime this weekly ritual was held in all ships and shore establishments of the Royal Navy and is probably designed as a window dressing. At the same time it never fails to boost the morale of the ship's company. To take part in these parades gives the individual a sense of pride, perhaps enough to increase one's height by at least one inch. With all ratings filed into two ranks each division would be commanded by its respective divisional officer. Envisage the Royal Marines paraded on the quarterdeck with their heads crowned in snow-white pith helmets and with brass buttons and silver instruments glistening in the brilliant sunlight of a still Sunday morning. Such splendour is unequalled by any other regiment in the world.

To the gentle strains of the now soft music the captain was starting to inspect the serried ranks of the ship's company. All this came to a sudden halt when an astonished Royal Marine drum major realised that he was now conducting a group of black and white minstrels. This was the result of a gigantic explosion erupting from the ship's funnel as a huge cloud of black smoke and oil residue in the shape of a monstrous sized mushroom drenched the entire parade. Looking down from the crow's-nest an observer would have witnessed a scene of utter confusion among the ranks below. Parallel to the turmoil on the upper-deck the scene in the boiler room could only be described as a re-enactment of Hal Roache's *Keystone Cops*. With the rattling ladders a never-ending cavalcade of personnel consisting of all ranks and denominations descended to the footplates below. Ahead of this convoy was the commander engineer who lost little time in showing his disapproval of the whole incident. Whilst he was bombarding the poor bewildered PO with questions, I withdrew to one side and gazed into space as one who was totally detached from everything that had happened. It was not for me to intervene while my overseer was taking the full blast of the commander's wrath. Although I had escaped a fearful lashing from the commander's tongue I was soon made aware that in his final analysis he had recognised the fact that I did at least make a small contribution to the upheaval. I was instantly relieved from my watch in the boiler room and given a transfer to the engine room. In his infinite wisdom the commander had reasoned that I would be less of a hazard to the ship if I was removed as far away from the boilers as possible, but alas any such notions would be very short-lived. However this new arrangement proved to be most pleasing to me as I now had a nice clean job and I was well out of reach of such retribution as I may have expected from my former PO for exposing him to such humiliation and embarrassment.

The after-effects of this disaster were not condemned by all of the ship's company. After all these were the days when the luxury of having automatic laundries aboard HM ships were just pipe dreams. With the absence of such amenities the task of washing clothes was fulfilled by nautical souls who, if offered sufficient compensation would dedicate their leisure hours to wallowing among the soapsuds in the ship's shower room. I recall my first acquaintance with such a firm. Soon after I joined the ship I had a few bits and pieces that needed washing, so with my arms loaded, I made my way towards the stokers' shower room and as I stepped into the doorway my eyes were drawn to a sight that I shall never forget. The place was empty save for one person who stood with his feet astride over a gigantic basin at the far end of the bathroom. As I walked towards him he stooped right down giving me a full view of his hairy arse. On his left cheek he had the letter 'I', on the other cheek the letter 'C' and down beside his anus the letter 'U'. 'I see you'.

What a place to put a tattoo, I thought, and how painful.

Meanwhile the demand for his services as a dhobi-wallah came as a windfall which he received like manna from heaven. The firm's financial rewards would be colossal.

Soon after, when the *Arethusa* was taking part in ma-noeuvres with the other ships of the squadron, a shipwright was boiling up some wax in the paint shop, when suddenly disaster struck as it boiled over and before a blink of an eyelid the paint shop became a blazing inferno. Because the store contained a large amount of inflammable material, Captain Vian went to investigate and was overcome by the fumes. Subsequently he was rescued by none other than the tattooed old sea-dog, who incidentally received no recognition for his bravery. This was because the captain was very dissatisfied with the fire party's performance and from then on fire drill became more regular than mealtimes. In the years to follow I was destined to meet up again with this old-timer during our service together in submarines. He was to earn my full respect and admiration. He was in fact one of the first submarine ratings to be awarded the DCM. That was all to happen three years later.

Before taking up my duties in the engine room I was given a guided tour. With one hand on my shoulder Petty Officer Rowland explained the workings of all the machinery, such as the circulating cooling systems, the compensating fresh water tank together with the extraction pump, which in the event of quick manoeuvres had to be started up immediately. From memory, I think the ideal level was three-quarters of a tank. A drastic reduction of speed would cause the level to rise at a very fast rate, this is when the extraction pump should be brought into operation. Failing to do so meant that water would pass over with steam, thereby wrecking the blades of the steam turbines.

All was well until one day, due to unexpected manoeuvres, the water level started to rise rapidly. Being completely oblivious of the situation, I did not notice that the water level had reached the top of the tank and was flooding across the plates in the engine room at a frightening rate. The next thing I knew was that a frantic PO of the watch went charging past me sending me sprawling into the surrounding machinery, whilst calling me all the foul names under the sun. He pounced on the extraction pump in great haste and turned on the operating switch. Needless to say once again I was in trouble.

The following day I was promoted to engineer's office messenger which many stokers considered to be the best job in the ship. As far as I was concerned it proved to be the easiest. Overalls had become a thing of the past and night watches non-existent. For the next few weeks my days were spent just sitting about the office and running the occasional message for the engineer commander. One of his whims that comes to mind was this: for his early morning shave I had to run down to the engine room and ask the evaporator watchkeeper for a mug full of distilled water. What difference that made to his looks, God only knows, but then again anything for a quiet life.

One morning after breakfast the commander stepped into the office and asked me to go down to the engine room and ask the officer of the watch for the salinometer reading. I now know that he wanted to know the amount of salt (if any) that may have been polluting the feed water. When I presented myself before the officer of the watch I made known to him the purpose of my mission. With an exaggerated highbrow accent he told me the reading and then added, 'All claw.' Not understanding what the poor man was saying I asked him to repeat it. Having made him repeat it no less than six times, I don't know who was most embarrassed, him or me. Still not knowing what he said, I gave it up as a bad job and withdrew from the engine room. Faced with the dilemma of explaining myself to the commander, I had reasoned that the only thing that I could do was to repeat the message in the same tone as it was given to me. Addressing the commander in my cockney accent I told him the salinometer reading, then in a faltering tone I added the rider, the feed water was 'all claw'. Having made me repeat the message over and over again the commander became more confused than I was. It wasn't long before his restraint gave way to intolerance as he brushed me aside and stormed out of the office to find out for himself. A few minutes later I heard him sharing the joke with another officer. 'What the poor man was saying was, that the feed water was clear, it may have helped if he had kept his false teeth in his mouth,' he said.

During the spring of 1938 the *Arethusa* lay at anchor off the coast of Barcelona.

By that time the so-called Insurgent Army had control of most of Spain leaving the Royalists besieged in Barcelona. One of our jobs was to pick up some of the women and children refugees and later transport them to Marseilles. I have no idea who these people were because they were all confined to the ship's recreation space where they were kept under strict guard leaving us no chance to communicate with them. Apart from these facts I could never fully understand the role of the Royal Navy in those hostile waters. Late in the afternoon while still at anchor several of us young sailors witnessed our first experience of war. The sound of distant explosions drew our attention to the skyline over the city, we could see what was said to be German and Italian bombers engaged in low level attacks only a mile or so away and judging from the absence of retaliation on the part of the Royalists it seemed to us that they were destined to defeat. At 10 a.m. the next day I was put in the unique position of setting foot on the shores of the besieged city of Barcelona. Whether or not the commander thought that I was a little bit more expendable than the rest of my shipmates I would never know, but for some reason or other I was one of three ratings detailed to be put ashore that morning. Dressed in a blue serge suit, belt and gaiters I was to accompany one officer and one signalman and another rating who I did not know. If anyone in the party knew why we were being sent ashore in a besieged city, they kept bloody quiet about it. Having landed not far from the city centre we climbed the stone steps, then turning westwards we walked a short distance along the sea wall until we came to a spot where a heliograph had been rigged. There the signalman, myself and the other rating waited while the officer in charge made off towards a large building which I could only guess housed staff of the

British Embassy or such like. He was probably making arrangements to evacuate them later that day. After an hour or so he returned to the sea wall and ordered the signalman to flash for a boat to be sent ashore to pick up whoever and take us all back to the ship. I am delighted to relate that not a drop of blood was shed, not even mine. One vivid memory I have of that day was of the well-constructed air raid shelters, a lesson I thought we should have learned far sooner than we did in our own war a year or so after. The same evening their cruiser *Baleares* put to sea and as she passed us on the starboard beam the *Arethusa*'s quartermaster's pipe summoned us to stand and salute the pride of the Spanish fleet. I remember standing on the upper deck returning the salutations of waving arms from hundreds of Spanish sailors. In just a few hours we were horrified to learn that the cruiser *Baleares* had been sunk by three Republican destroyers and a heavy loss of life was suspected. Although I had seen photographs of our own destroyer *Hunter*, when she had hit a mine a year earlier, this was the first time that the reality of war had been brought home to me.

Soon after Barcelona fell, the *Arethusa* withdrew from Spanish waters. Then having been told that our next port of call would be off the French Riviera the ship's company was eagerly awaiting shore leave. For many of us it was the first time abroad and having been given a glimpse of sights to see by more travelled hands, we couldn't wait to get to grips with new experiences.

It so happened that while at anchor off Villa Franc, the following announcement sounded over the ship's tannoy: 'This is Admiral Wells speaking, I shall be pacing the quarterdeck between 1700 and 1800 hours for the next two evenings, if any man in this ship does not know me, he is to come along and have a real good look at me.' Although it did occur to me that I did not know what he looked like, I paid little or no attention to the Admiral's plea, and so I dismissed all ideas of taking part in these observations, after all I had two years to find out what he looked like.

At 1800 hours the following evening the Regulating Chief Stoker sent for me. 'Have you been up to look at the Admiral yet?' he asked.

'No Chief,' I replied.

'You are well advised to do so at once. In case you don't know, this whole exercise is for your benefit,' he snapped. He then went on to say that I and my shore-going oppo had embarrassed the Admiral by sauntering into the midst of a party of dignitaries who were accompanied by him on the promenade in Cannes. Apart from the fact that we ignored his presence by not saluting, he was not impressed by our general appearance, the wearing of hats flat-a-back is not done in the presence of admirals.

The Chief Stoker's dressing down left me no alternative, I now had to pay a visit to the quarterdeck. I timidly peered round the corner and as I did so the piercing eyes of Admiral Wells stopped me dead in my tracks. I instantly became aware that the Admiral had not mistaken my identity. The scowl that appeared across his brow immediately indicated that he had marked my card for life. When the *Arethusa* returned to Malta, my days as office messenger came to an abrupt end. It would seem that no matter where I was placed I was a constant pain in the arse as far as the Chief Stoker was concerned.

He had tried giving me the easiest and cleanest job in the ship and that didn't work, so now he was going to try me out on the hardest and dirtiest one.

'You,' said the Chief Stoker, 'will be joining the funnel party, that means you have been given the job of cleaning the inside of the ship's funnel.'

This filthy job had become almost bearable due to the presence of a comical friend who answered to the name

Ginger Larking. This young lad from Birmingham was always out for a bit of fun. In charge of the party was a petty officer, Wilf Scarf. He was as good humoured as one could imagine an ex-Grimsby trawlerman to be. During the morning Ginger tried to brighten up our lot with a little mirth. Choosing Petty Officer Scarf as his victim, he waited for him to get within hearing range.

Turning towards me Ginger said, 'Do you remember my mate on the *Penelope*, Tom?'

'Yes of course I do,' I answered.

Then raising his voice a little louder, Ginger said, 'Two months ago he was cleaning the top of the *Penelope*'s funnel when he slipped and fell to the bottom. They found him there with his brains bashed in.'

Wilf went for the bait like a hungry shark. 'What rotten luck,' he gasped.

'Yeah,' said Ginger. 'He seemed quite happy when I visited him in hospital because they made him a petty officer.'

Then amidst shrieks of laughter Scarf chased the pair of us round the gantry using all the foul language he could think of.

After spending a week or so in harbour, we were once again heading for the open sea. Rumour had it that we were joining the rest of the squadron for gunnery practice. Normally I was a good sailor at sea but due to a heavy booze-up the night before, it became necessary for me to ask permission to leave the boiler room in order to use the heads. I hurried up the ladder and continued racing towards the heads having reached them in the nick of time I dived into the first cubicle and dropped my pants. As I gasped with relief the whole place lit up, as a thunderous flash that almost split my head in two. Not waiting to finish, I pulled up my overalls and made a dash for the doorway. As I did so the ghost-like figure of the gunner's mate loomed up before me. On seeing me he became more frantic than I was.

He came running towards me like a mad bull and as he glared through the visor of his anti-flash headgear he bawled out, 'What the hell do you think you are doing up here? Get to hell out of it. What are you, some sort of a lunatic?'

'How was I to know that you were about to let go a full broadside with those bloody great guns just above my head,' I answered.

When I returned to the boiler room, the chief stoker was grinning all over his chops as he shouted in my ear, 'Do you feel better now?'

'Yes but I could have done without the bloody laxative,' I shouted back at him. For once in my life I couldn't see the funny side of it.

In order to establish a reconciliation between Great Britain and Italy, their Lordships decided to dispatch our ship on a courtesy visit to Venice. This was because prior to the summer of 1938, goodwill between our two countries had been marred due to our government's disapproval of Italy's war on Abyssinia. To improve relations it was now time to extend a hand of friendship towards our former adversaries. With our ship moored directly adjacent to St Mark's Square, it would seem that we were chosen to play a major role in this exercise. It was therefore imperative that our ship's company should maintain a high standard of good behaviour, especially while on shore.

To discourage wanton frolicking by well-meaning, liberated sailors, six junior ratings, including myself, were detailed for picket duties ashore, but because our ships had not visited Italian shores for over two years, none of us knew the layout of the local terrain.

To rectify this problem it was decided that a squad of Italian pickets would accompany us. It would be perfectly plausible for one to expect that this inspired tactical ploy would ensure that their Lordships' dream of Utopia would be fulfilled. At 1600 hours on the day of our arrival. The *Arethusa*'s motor boat disembarked us six selected ambassadors of peace, goodwill and tranquillity. After climbing a few steps in front of St Mark's Square we stood and gazed in awe at the perfect line-up of the Italian squad. They were like guards. There was no way that we were prepared to even try to compete with their smart presentation. As we reached them, the leading hand in charge of us told us to form two ranks and fall in beside them. Then hearing the Italian equivalent to 'right turn, quick march' we staggered on behind them. With each few steps the gap between the two squads became ever-increasing as the Italians marched along at a pace that would have put a light infantry regiment to shame.

'What is the hurry?' we shouted out to the Italians, but they still kept racing down the street.

'Can we stop at one of the bars for a drink?' we asked our leading hand. By this time it seemed that the whole arrangement was getting out of hand, these Italians were taking their job far too seriously as far as we were concerned. Then deciding enough was enough, we left our now distant escort at the next bar that we came to. After pointing to them where we were going we invited them to join us but to our amazement they refused. Instead they came to a halt, then turned back and remained standing in two ranks outside the bar. A long wait of at least two hours would dispel any notion that they may have had of us rejoining them. Bewildered by what they believed was our carefree attitude towards our duties, they turned tail and made tracks back to their quarters, where no doubt they made full report about the wayward behaviour of the *Arethusa*'s picket patrol.

Later that evening our little party was brought to an

abrupt ending. The barking commands of 'Fall in outside at the double,' brought my attention to a figure standing in the bar's entrance, and through my bleary eyes I espied the chief regulator backed up by a second picket patrol. It became quite evident that this lot meant business. Their orders were to escort us back to the ship at once. Through the veil of passing years I cannot remember the reception we received after we were taken back to the ship. What I do remember the whole incident came to a sudden climax when our ship returned to Malta. As for Leading Stoker Fowler who was in charge of our patrol I never did find out what happened to him. All I knew about him, was that he was a most inoffensive character who never had put a foot wrong in his Navy career, what chance did he have with people like me to encourage him along a wayward path.

No sooner had the *Arethusa* moored up to its buoys in Singale Creek when a messenger appeared on the mess-deck, 'Shattock you are on draft to the UK,' he informed me. So together with my pal Chippy and another two ratings we began to pack our kits all ready to join the battleship *Repulse* which was to be homeward bound that evening.

On joining the massive battleship the four of us were guided to a large mess-deck. I was quite surprised to find myself in company with forty other ratings who like me had suddenly been drafted from various other ships throughout the fleet. As I settled down with my new mess-mates, the conversation turned towards the reason for us to be given a sudden draft home. I remember becoming quite indignant when one knowing character had the audacity to suggest that we were all undesirable and that we were being sent home to some dark corner where we would no longer embarrass their Lordships.

Knowing little about my companions I began to wonder if there could be a grain of truth in this assertion. After all, was it coincidence that one of the other three of my partners from the *Arethusa* happened to be the same guy who was with me when we failed to salute the Admiral. Still at the back of my mind was the vivid imprint of the Admiral's scowl which I knew I would carry to my grave. I was now fully convinced that I at least was one to whom the Admiral owed no favours.

During the voyage home I became friendly with a jovial character who responded to the name Nobby. Almost every ship in the Royal Navy must have carried at least one Nobby Hall, with most of them bearing a striking resemblance in character and personality to each other. Could it be that having been blessed with such a name, that their carefree images were something that they worked on? Whatever the reason this guy came from the perfect mould, he was graced with that kind of jovial and friendly attitude that I came to admire. With his wit and humour he was able to create roars of laughter in the midst of perhaps the most serious situations. In a nutshell he was fun to be with. Sometimes during a hushed silence he would burst into song, one of his favourites was the old Navy ballad well known to seafarers. 'My name is Nobby Hall, bless them all,' etc. These foul lyrics could sound most disturbing to the ears of virgin sailors, but such souls being a rare commodity, no one was bothered. During my short acquaintance with Nobby, he told me that he had volunteered for service in submarines. Although I thought that he was crazy I did respect his zest for adventure, but the factor that aroused my interest most of all, was the financial advantage offered to such adventurers.

Shortly after returning to Chatham Barracks from foreign service leave I once again met up with Nobby. This time he was most excited because he had just been called to report to the drafting office with his kit bag and hammock. From there he was to be sent to HMS *Dolphin* for submarine training. After lending him a hand with his kit he succeeded in persuading me to volunteer for submarines.

My last memory of that brief encounter was a farewell wave as he disappeared into the back of a truck which was to take him to Chatham railway station. During the years to follow I never ceased looking out for him, but fate had it we were never to meet again. The next morning I was drafted to the destroyer *Whirlwind*. After being told that she was in the reserve fleet and that she was tied up in No. 2 basin in Chatham dockyard I was looking forward to a few week-ends in my home town, Southend. As I climbed the gangway I was deafened by the sound of riveting. The steel decks were littered with pneumatic hoses which were reaching out in all directions. With the dockyard maties swarming like bees all over the ship, the old tub didn't look like the man-of-war that I expected to see. As I stood and took these activities into account I became very conscious of the apparent urgency of the progress. In fact it was only a matter of days before this ghost ship sprang to life and was taking part in Britain's most formidable fleet review of 1938 at Spithead.

Soon after Chamberlain's announcement, 'Peace in our time', the *Whirlwind* returned to Chatham and I was transferred to the destroyer *Whitley*. The crew of this ship consisted mostly of reserve veterans who had been mobilised for the 1938 September crisis. They were a jolly crowd who seemed to regard their recall more like a holiday than for real. Among them, there was a small scattering of regulars like myself. One such member was a young sprog (second class stoker) and this was his first ship. Being very good-looking he was quickly taken under the wing of an old three badge man. The fun started one day when Stripey offered the young stoker his plum duff and custard. The jibes that followed were meant and taken as a joke which seemed to escalate day by day, when the old-timer continued to forego his precious afters in order to keep in the youngster's good books. Every mealtime the youngster would return from the boiler room to find his place at the table had been meticulously prepared with a knife, fork and spoon and placed carefully in position together with the essential condiments.

Eventually this mock courtship became so serious that we decided some thing had to be done to make the affair legal. Now what could be more entertaining than a wedding. So it came to pass the bans were read out loud and clear and then pinned to the ship's notice board. Then came the long-awaited day for this wonderful occasion. The young lad was dressed in a white dress which was salvaged from the engine room rag bag, his head was adorned in a beautiful white veil made from an old net curtain. As the two splendid sports stood before a packed audience on the stokers' mess-deck each responded to the solemn vows dictated by the senior leading stoker wearing a dog-collar cut out of white cardboard. All was going well until he pulled rank by claiming the first kiss from the blushing bride. Stripey didn't like it one little bit. To conclude the ceremony the old sea-daddy placed a bone ring on the youngster's finger while the hushed congregation exploded into hearty cheers. A specially made wedding cake was cut into fifteen slices and we all sat down to morning tea.

Later that afternoon we all went ashore and continued to celebrate the momentous occasion. Just to put the record straight all this is written with tongue in cheek, I am quite certain that this was not a gay relationship, the whole scenario was just a little bit of fun upheld by two good sports. Such antics did help to while away the time, so for a short term we could almost forget the austerity that surrounded us. During 1941 I was destined to meet up with the then, not so young lad who had also joined submarines but like so many of my friends was lost soon after.

I regard my time on the *Whitley* during the spring cruise of 1939 as some of the most gruelling experiences of rough weather that I was ever to witness during my twelve years at sea. I feel quite sure that anyone who took part in those manoeuvres would agree that the high seas were atrocious. Despite the conditions the ship's company from the captain down were relentless in their aim to achieve wartime standards of life at sea on a destroyer. One incident that remains clear in my mind was one evening after climbing out of the airlock doors I saw a warrant officer hanging on to a lifeline with one hand and holding his cheek with the other.

Apparently instinct had overruled his better judgement during a vain effort to stop the motor boat from being washed over the side by a tremendous wave. The whole of his cheek was sliced clean open.

Sometime during early June the *Whitley* returned to Chatham where most of her crew paid off. As for myself I was drafted to yet another ship in the reserve fleet, this time it was the cruiser *Dragon* which was tied up at the far end of No. 2 basin near to St Mary's island. As I struggled up the gangway with my kit bag and hammock my thoughts immediately returned to the day I joined the *Whirlwind*, and as I stepped over the maze of pneumatic pipes I felt as though I had stepped back in time.

Then raising my voice so that I could be heard above the din created by the riveting I shouted to one of the work-men, 'Can you tell me the way to the stokers' mess?'

Pointing forward he answered, 'Walk through the cov-ered way and go down the second hatch that you come to.'

My new mess-mates consisted of a few one badge men and a sprinkling of old-timers. They were a happy bunch of chaps and I can only look back and regard the time spent with them as some of the happiest times I had known.

Apart from the boiler cleaning, life on the ship was very cushy. Even that would have been bearable had we a heated bath to step into afterwards, instead we had to manage with a wash down from a bucket of hot water on the mess-deck. Other than that there was little else to do. Nothing ever being perfect, there was to be another chore that worried me. With all boilers shut down in the ship, steam for heating water for officers' baths and the galley had to be supplied by a donkey boiler which stood on the jetty abreast of the quarterdeck. All was well until it became my turn to keep watch on it. This being the first time that I had ever been called upon to shovel coal into a boiler, I asked one of the old-timers what to do. He responded by taking me over to the boiler where he explained how everything worked.

'There is nothing much to worry about,' he said. 'Just make sure that you keep half a glass of water on the gauge and the correct head of steam.' He then told me that the boiler had to be shut down at 2300 hours each night. He then explained how the fire had to be pushed to the back and banked up ready to spread at 0530 the following morning. Not forgetting to top up the boiler with water. I suppose it was about midnight before I turned into my hammock, but not for long. My peaceful sleep was soon disturbed by the sound of the quartermaster descending the ladder in leaps and bounds.

'Where is the duty Stoker?' he screamed out.

Then putting my head over the side of my hammock, 'That's me,' I replied. 'What is the cause of all that noise out there?'

'It's your bloody boiler, it's pulsating so violently it's doing the polka up and down the jetty,' he answered. I immediately jumped out of my hammock and went racing towards the red-hot glowing cylinder which was about to blow up at any moment. I then looked for the longest steel slice available, but even with that extended at arm's length to unhinge the boiler door I still suffered a badly scorched face, arms and hair. Then with the furnace door open I kept making repeated attempts to get near enough to draw the fire from the grid, but each time I tried I was forced back because of the heat, my face and arms were burning but I still kept at it until eventually the red-hot coals had all been raked free from the boiler. I then pumped more feed water into the boiler and waited patiently for the boiler to cool down.

It was 0300 before I climbed back into my hammock, but not to sleep. The soreness that I suffered because of my scorched body together with the worry of having to flash up the boiler in order to provide steam for the various services required, was sufficient to give me insomnia. These things gave me plenty to think about until it was time for me to light up again. Although I allowed myself plenty of time for the boiler to work up a good head of steam, it somehow failed to do so and by 0900 I had people shouting and screaming words of abuse at me from all directions. If only they had been around at midnight when I had enough steam to send the whole fleet into battle, I thought.

I made many blunders during my first few years of service but I choose to gratify my ego by claiming that I seldom made the same mistake twice. Had I done so I think that the world's most formidable fleet of the time would have suffered more dents and bruises that the Admiralty could have provided for. With people like me in the Navy who needs a war!

By mid-August 1939 my steam-easy days in the reserved fleet had ended and the *Dragon* was ready to take up duties on a wartime footing. Considering that most of her crew consisted of recalled reservists and pensioners, some of whom had been in civvy street since the end of the First World War, this was a remarkable achievement. It was during my first wartime watch in the engine room when I asked the Chief ERA how long did he think it would be before we went into battle. Being a First World War veteran, I thought that he would know the answer. I remember how relieved I was when he told me that it could be months before we ran into the enemy. From September until just before Christmas we aboard the *Dragon* spent patrolling the North Atlantic Ocean. Our job was to intercept all merchant ships bound for German-occupied Europe and bring them back to Scapa Flow.

After four months on these patrols the *Dragon*'s Captain Bowes Lyon addressed the ship's company. The theme of his speech was related to the urgent need for recruitment of young officers and ratings into the submarine service. The following day many of us youngsters found ourselves on draft to Chatham. At the time I had no reason to associate the two incidents but I was soon to learn that the events that followed were the direct result of the captain's speech. Contrary to the thoughts that I had about my own destination, one of my friends and mess-mates called Jack Whiting knew exactly where he was going. Having listened to the captain's appeal for volunteers for service in submarines he immediately signed on the dotted line. At the time I thought he was crazy but no matter what I said to discourage him, nothing was going to alter his decision.

For the two of us, the journey south became a nightmare, first there was a sea trip to the mainland, then a long coach drive to the nearest railway station, after that another change to a second rail station. Besides having to hump our own kit, Whiting and I got lumbered with thirty tool boxes belonging to ERAs, who sat back like lords and didn't lift a finger to help us as we humped their boxes from one form of transport to another. Some of them was so bloody heavy that I swear that they must have brought half the *Dragon*'s main engines with them.

The day after our arrival at Chatham, Whiting and I

were sitting in the mess when the tannoy blurted out the following order, 'Stoker Whiting to muster outside the drafting office with his kitbag and hammock.' As for Jack's response I couldn't understand it, he was as pleased as a dog with two tails. I sat and watched as he packed his kit while all the time I was calling him all the names I could think of. You must be mad I kept on saying.

It was about 1100 hours when I stood by the tailboard of the truck that was to take him to the station, then just as it pulled away I waved him goodbye just as I did to Nobby Hall a year before. Within an hour of my friend's departure I too was summoned to the drafting office, then as I stepped up on to the platform in front of the window a voice within said, 'Stoker Shattock you are on draft to HMS *Dolphin*.'

Then not realising the significance of what he was saying, I turned and walked away, and just as the penny dropped I turned in my tracks saying, 'That's not to join submarines, is it?'

'That is right,' he answered. 'You volunteered a year ago, I have your name down here.'

'But there was not a war on then, I'm not going in a submarine,' I said to him.

'Well, I wish it was me, I would love to be back in them,' was his reply. 'Why don't you give it a try, you will get three weeks' training with each weekend off, then if you don't pass the course they will send you back here.' Keeping the chief's parting words in mind, I planned to do exactly that, fail the course.

At 1800 hours I boarded the pinnace that was awaiting our arrival by the steps at HMS *Vernon*, at Portsmouth, it was teeming with rain and altogether I felt utterly miserable. A few minutes later I was standing on top of the steps in front of Fort Blockhouse just staring into the gloomy shadows of the ancient structure and thinking how forbidding it all seemed to be.

I am going to hate every moment that I am in this place, I thought to myself. After reporting to the chief regulator and various other officials, I finally found my way into the submarine training mess and as I walked across the room I came face to face with Jack Whiting.

'You cunning bugger, you knew all the time that you were going into subs,' he shouted.

Although Jack had arrived only an hour or so before I did he had already been issued with his submarine sweater and was proudly wearing it. During the remaining part of the evening, Jack gave me a summary of the training routine and pointed out to me one or two interesting characters, one of whom was chalking the scores of a game of darts in the corner. He was a tall lean man which explained his nickname.

Pointing to him, Jack said, 'That's Snaky, he is the brother of Leading Stoker Arnold who escaped from the submarine *Thetis*.'

Laughing while trying to convince him that it was no wish of mine to be there, I answered, 'You picked a bloody fine time to remind me about that.'

The *Thetis* was an ill-fated submarine which came to its end when on trials a year earlier, thereby trapping one hundred and five men leaving all but three entombed in the depths below. The tragedy happened when the torpedo officer ordered one of the internal tube doors to be opened. Before doing so the operator had to check that the external door was shut and the tube was dry. He does this by opening a drain cock; if no rush of water is forthcoming it can be assumed that it is safe to open the inside door. Unknown to the operator, a painter had been at work with bitumen which had flowed into the drain hole thereby clogging it up, so that when it was tested it unfortunately gave a false indication. With the bow door open there was a twenty-one inch diameter hole open to the sea. Thus the torpedo space and fore-end compartment became flooded in seconds. After being trapped for hours Captain Orran, Leading Stoker Arnold, and a civilian dockyard worker made a successful escape. There would have been more but a fourth member of the crew got his legs trapped in the upper hatch of the escape chamber leaving those still inside unable to shut it down to make ready for the next four to escape. From there after the submarine escape method using the chamber was abandoned in favour of the twill trunk system which was not nearly so complicated as using the chamber.

The twenty-one day course passed all too soon and when it came to the final exam, instead of failing I passed with top marks, but that did not help me on the last day when I almost failed the escape tank. Although I was a good swimmer, for some reason I could not get used to breathing from a bag under water. The escape drill in those days seemed very primitive to that of today. Below the eighteen-foot tank an identical escape chamber to one inside a submarine was fixed. First of all the instructor told us about the Davis escape breathing bag. Stripped down to our swimming trunks the bag was hung about our chest by means of a strap around the neck with the lower part of it secured around the waist by another strap. Oxygen was supplied to the lungs by means of a small bottle fixed to the bottom of the bag. Sticking out from the front of the bag there was a tube to which a mouthpiece and a shut-off cock is attached.

The drill was as follows. First you charge the bag with a burst of oxygen. Insert the mouthpiece and at the same time open the shut-off cock on the breathing tube thus freeing the passage of oxygen from the bag to the lungs. Put on the nose clip which is tied to the breathing tube. When breathing comfortably step into the chamber. Shut the watertight door and flood the chamber; while doing so, wet the eye goggles and wear them. Water will stop flooding when the trapped air above its surface becomes compressed equal to that of the sea pressure. Then open the vent in the hatch to allow the trapped air to escape. Doing so will allow the flood water to rise until it reaches the hatch. Only then is it safe to open the hatch and make your ascent. Before doing so there is another must. Open the exhaust valve on the bottom of the bag, then making sure to keep clear of the jumping wire, start your ascent. To avoid the risk of getting the bends, slow down your ascent by holding out at arm's length the apron which is attached to the bag. When reaching the surface, shut off the cock on the breathing tube and the exhaust valve. Remove the mouthpiece and at the same time check that the bag is sufficiently buoyant by giving it another burst of oxygen from the bottle, and then wait to be picked up. Neglect to do any one of those things then you will drown.

The lucky few who have made a successful escape using the Davis apparatus is overshadowed by the large number of men who have drowned while trying to do so. It is my opinion hurried training must take a large share of the blame. Had I myself had the misfortune to have been placed in the position of having to have made an escape I feel sure that my one or two hours' training would have paid for a first class ticket to Davy Jones's locker room. It was not until after the war was over that I was given the chance on several occasions to make an escape from the training tank. However having struggled through the tank training and receiving the benefits of submarine pay there was to be no turning back. The following morning I was on draft to Rosyth.

Chapter Three

Into the Unknown

At the outbreak of the Second World War the RN possessed no more than sixty submarines, many of which could only be described as old crocks, outdated and well overdue for the knacker's yard. Recognition must be given to the brave men who crewed these vessels. They revealed outstanding courage to even venture outside harbour let alone in attempting the audacious missions that they were assigned to undertake. These men were the first to be given the task of penetrating the dreadful minefields which guarded the sanctuaries of the enemy. In spite of overwhelming odds against them, these early veterans did a marvellous job by sinking a large number of enemy ships and thereby filling in the gap until such time as the Navy was to boast a large fleet of modern boats, such as the 'T' class submarines.

It was inevitable that many of these elderly boats did not return from their patrols. One by one the fate of these boats together with our brave comrades would be made known to those of us who remained behind. As the toll mounted, my mind became numb with disbelief as to what was happening. These men who I was privileged to have known were worthy of all the praise that one could bestow on them. They were brave men who kept the submarine service together during the first three months of the war. Their successes were vital. Without such men the splendid record of what was to follow would never had been documented. Their determination and dogged approach in the face of adversity was to inspire all of us who followed in their wake.

By the time I had finished my training the urgency for replacement submarine crews had become apparent. Recent losses had taken a heavy toll of trained submariners. This desperate situation left us newcomers with no other alternative, we had to be thrown in at the deep end. After completing our three weeks training on a Friday it came as no surprise for us to be drafted to the submarine parent ship the very next day. Its name we were told was HMS *Forth* which was moored up in Rosyth dockyard in Scotland.

Although I felt apprehensive as to my future, I cannot say that I felt any regret about leaving the training mess in Platypus hut, Fort Blockhouse. The building must have been at least a hundred years old. The only comfort afforded was a long mess table between two equally long bench seats which at night-time became dimly illuminated by one solitary twenty watt bulb suspended from the ceiling. To me at that time, it seemed like the most inhospitable place in the world but in the years to follow I would have given anything to have been there again.

For the whole of Saturday I and five others from my class travelled north to Rosyth in Scotland, as for the other three lads in the class they had been drafted to an operational submarine in the south. I regret to say that their fate was decided within a few days of our departure. They were lost on their very first patrol. We arrived on board the *Forth* just in time for supper and by the time we had eaten and transferred our kits to our allocated lockers we were ready to turn in for the night. I was awakened next morning by the sound of piano music which became dominated by a woman's voice. She was calling out drill instructions.

'Up, one, two, three... Down, one, two, three...' and so on. At the time, the BBC broadcast such a programme at six thirty in the morning. Although I did not partake in the exercises I found the accompanying music both lively and stimulating.

Unlike Fort Blockhouse the whole atmosphere of my new surroundings made me feel secure and relaxed. Discipline was less severe so that a few minutes' lie-in did not go amiss. As I lay nice and snug in my hammock, I thought how happy I would be if I could spend the rest of the war in these comfortable surroundings. Although the war was only five months old I had spent no less than three months on the North Atlantic patrols aboard HMS *Dragon* so perhaps such thoughts could be excusable. Later that morning I was put to work on one of the new 'T' class submarines. I was soon to discover that this newly built vessel was equipped to carry mines. These mines were housed inside the saddle tanks and could be released from the submerged position. This operation in itself, I should have thought would have been a delicate manoeuvre, as one could imagine with strong undercurrents, one little tilt or an obstruction the whole lot would be blown to kingdom come.

Whilst on its first patrol, this submarine had been trapped inside the Norwegian fjords and depth-charged for forty-two hours. Although the deepest reading on the depth-gauge showed a reading of 500 feet I was well assured that for one period the depth in the after-ends was 600 feet. The fact that all the dog-teeth round the watertight door had been filed down was plainly visible, therefore I was convinced that it was true. The whole of the one inch thick steel surrounding door frame had been distorted by the immense sea pressure. During the attack, the men in the after-ends became imprisoned when the watertight door became jammed in the shut position and it took them a long time to get it open again. The enemy had kept in such close contact for so long that the Chief Engineer Warrant Officer Stevens suspected that large lumps of grease used to lubricate the mines release equipment, had floated to the surface, thereby giving away the boat's position. Having compared the advantages and disadvantages of these mines it was decided to unship them and clean off all the grease from the inside of the saddle tanks. This task provided myself and two others with two days work. Then as soon as the tanks were cleaned the previously hinged flaps which provided the mines exit were welded in the shut position and sealed off for ever.

The submarine's name was the *Tetrarch* and was recognised by what I thought to be the lucky number seventy-seven. During this time I had worked with a number of the *Tetrarch* stokers, of whom many were still in their early teens. Although they were very young men, such was their experience that in one patrol they had become seasoned veterans in submarine warfare. I had taken an instant liking to this crowd, so much so that I expressed my desire to join them, but alas for the time being they had their full compliment and no one else was needed. The same evening I was sitting alone in the spare-crew's mess, with my hands cupped under my chin I was just staring into blank space. Suddenly I caught the eye of another lone sailor sitting at the opposite table. A badge on his arm depicting crossed flags denoting that he was a bunting-tosser (a signalman).

He looked at me and shouted over, 'What's the matter stokes? You look chocker.'

'I would like to go ashore but I am broke,' I answered.

'That's no trouble,' was his reply. He then walked towards me and placed a pound note on my table saying, 'I can't go anywhere so you may as well have it.' Bear in mind that it was the first time that we had set eyes on each other I thought it was a very friendly and trusting gesture, such as I had never experienced in other communities. I am sorry to relate I knew him just long enough to repay him and learn that he answered to the name Cock Hoys.

The following evening I was getting ready to go ashore when I was approached by the regulating chief's messenger. He looked at me and said inquiringly, 'Stoker Shattock?'

'Yes that's me,' I answered.

'Report to the drafting office,' he said. Then as I turned to walk away, he whispered in my ear, *Tetrarch*.'

The drafting coxswain confirmed my draft by telling me to collect my steaming kit and report to the coxswain of the *Tetrarch* immediately. He then said that the boat was alongside and was ready to put to sea.

Of course the days of steam-driven submarines had long gone, but for some reason or other the Navy is always reluctant to depart with its old terminology. Just for the record I packed two newly issued submarine sweaters with long johns to match, two shifts of vests and underpants and two pair of socks. I would like to add that before the patrol was over I would be wearing the whole lot at one time. Although I was disappointed because I was unable to go ashore, my mind became fully occupied with a mixture of excitement and fear of the unknown. Would I be able to cope with the confinement within a submarine? Even more worrying to me, was the inevitable depth-charging that would surely be testing my metal before long.

As I reminisce now, I can vividly recall how the strain of putting on a brave face was almost as terrifying as death itself. If these were the thoughts of such as I whose duties were comparatively menial, I shudder to think of the terrifying strain the captain must endure while attacking or being attacked. This is the time when the eyes of every hand in the control room would be focused on him. He would be fully aware that any sign of weakness would be noticed immediately, any indecision would have demoralising consequences among the crew. However at that time I had little or no knowledge of the respect such men would earn.

As I stepped to the top of the gangway leading down to the *Tetrarch* I noticed someone with a camera. Paying no concern as to what he was doing I pushed past and made my way down the steps. It was not until two years after, while serving in the Mediterranean Sea, I flipped over the pages of a *Reader's Digest* and there on the back page I saw a picture of a lone sailor about to enter the fore hatch of a 'T' class submarine. Underneath the photograph was printed the caption: 'A submariner proceeding on patrol at Rosyth.' Although it was only the back view, I instantly recognised myself.

After negotiating my footsteps down a steep ladder into the fore-ends one of the hands immediately secured the hatch shut behind me and so making me aware that I was the last man to step aboard.

At the foot of the ladder there was barely room to stand, the compartment was crammed full with stores. There were cases of eggs, butter, soup, tinned fruit, bags of potatoes, greens and all sorts of provisions to keep fifty-four men alive for the next eighteen days. Space was so vital that bread had to be stored in hammocks which were slung from the deck-heads. How and where a dozen seamen could find space to sleep I never ceased to wonder. However, the reality of their plight occupied no place in my thoughts at the time. My first steps took me through the elliptic shaped hatch, then past the crew space to the chiefs' and POs' mess. When reaching the latter I poked my head through the drawn curtains and asked for the coxswain. My eyes focused on a stockily built man who was seated near to the gangway. His ruddy cheeks and broad set features gave him an air of dignity to support him for the office in which he was employed. I had made no mistake, he was indeed the coxswain.

Looking up from his preoccupation he exclaimed, 'Ah, you must be the new stoker. You are just in time.' He then took from a folder a next-of-kin form and handing it to me said, 'Get this filled in at once and return it to me.'

Realising the urgency of his request I complied with his wishes and completed the form there and then. Taking the document from me he disappeared from the mess and left me under the charge of the chief stoker who was sitting on the other side of the table. In contrast to the coxswain he was a slimly built man. His chiselled features and once dark hair which was highlighted by streaks of iron grey portrayed a fine character. Had it been peacetime this worthy veteran would be counting the days to enjoying his pension. But in spite of his long service in the Navy he had lost none of his Tyneside Geordie accent. In an easy-going manner he proceeded to show me my position on the watch rota and pointed out that my duties would be confined to the after-ends. I took an instant liking to this man and time alone would reveal my judgement to be true.

Leaving the noticeboard, he said, 'Follow me.' Our tour took us past the ERA's mess, the ward-room, control room, galley, wireless office, engine room, motor room, the stokers' mess then finally the after-ends. He then introduced me to a friendly man who was well past his prime.

'This is Stoker Steverson, anything that you want to know Stevo will put you right.'

Then with a broad grin the old-timer replied, 'Who is going to show me?' His reply did not dismay the chief stoker one little bit. He knew him of old, the two of them had served together in submarines many years prior to the outbreak of war. Being the oldest veteran in the boat, his guidance was of immense value to the rest of us whose average age was less than twenty years. Following a loud click on the tannoy we heard the order 'Harbour stations, secure for leaving harbour.' For those of us remaining below were left the tasks of securing the dog-clips to the hatches on the pressure hull, packing away the crocks, tying down buckets and other bits and pieces. In reply to the motor room telegraph I watched the LTOs make the switches 'Slow Ahead' and so we edged our way from the protection of the mother ship. Within a few minutes both main motors having progressed to half speed ahead, the *Tetrarch* slid silently through the exit of the basin and disappeared into the night.

On reaching the open sea both main motors were stopped and the main engine clutches engaged, then with a deafening roar both main engines sprang to life. Very soon the orders 'Diving stations, uncotter main vents,' blurted out over the tannoy.

'We are now preparing for the trim dive,' Stevo advised me. The purpose of this preliminary dive was to allow the first lieutenant to make exacting adjustments to the trim or balance of the submerged vessel.

A question that I have often been asked is, 'What is it like in a submarine and how does it work?' For this reason I will endeavour to enlighten such people. To obtain the maximum efficiency regarding the manoeuvrability of a submerged vessel, it has to be only just negative buoyancy. One can appreciate that changeable conditions such as the usage of fuel or the shipping aboard of provisions causes the weight of the boat to be constantly changing. To rectify this, compensating tanks are fitted at strategic points throughout the boat so that when stores are used, the ocean provides the necessary weight of water to compensate for it. When stores are taken aboard the procedure is reversed; instead of flooding in, the water is pumped out. The responsibility for this job falls upon the first lieutenant who is forever vigilant of the changing needs. As one would expect, the major changes take place just before the submarine puts to sea. Experience has proved it is always necessary to have a trim dive before proceeding on a wartime patrol.

With the boom defence being closed behind us the boat was now heading in a north-easterly direction with all its crew closed up for diving. Suddenly the five lookouts, the officer of the watch and the captain hastily descended through the conning tower hatch on to the control room deck. The captain, who was the last man down, shut the hatch and pressed the klaxon. The outside ERA who was stationed on the diving panel snapped open the six main vent levers, then with a hiss of escaping air the boat dived. The captain then ordered the two hydroplane operators to maintain the depth of thirty-two feet and directed the outside ERA to shut main vents. Within a short space of time and only a slight adjustment to the water levels in the compensating tanks, the fact that the first lieutenant had got his sums right was confirmed. The captain, who in the meantime had been scanning the skies and surface through the forehead periscope, satisfied himself that all was clear, and gave the orders, 'Down periscope, stand by to surface.' In reply to his next order, 'Blow all main ballast tanks,' the panel operator swung open the HP air master blow valve, then a hiss of air followed by a sudden bump, the boat surfaced. On breaking surface the captain immediately opened the coning tower hatch and leaped to the bridge, close on his heels followed the officer of the watch and the five lookouts. In the meantime the order, 'Open LP master blows, and start the blower,' was given by the first lieutenant. Next came the order, 'Flood "Q" tank.' The panel operator then snapped open the appropriate lever observing the green light warning indicator and reported back to the captain, '"Q" tank flooded.'

The captain then ordered, 'Shut "Q" Kingston, fall out

diving stations, patrol routine.' Here I take leave to explain to the lay reader that 'Q' tank is a large tank and when flooded together with the main ballast tanks enables the submarine to reach depths of fifty feet in just fifty-eight seconds. With the ever increasing attacks from the air, any hope of survival made quick diving essential. With her nose pointing in a north-easterly direction the *Tetrarch* was headed towards those dreaded minefields which guarded the entrance to the Kattegat. It would be about this time when the captain would be opening his sealed orders for his assigned mission.

It had been explained to me that as soon as we arrived in our patrolling area, all daylight hours would have to be spent beneath the surface. It would be most unwise for chef to cook a midday meal under these conditions because the ovens would soon burn up the precious oxygen within the boat. This was one very good reason for changing our nights into days. A few of us would sit in the mess peeling potatoes and preparing the vegetables for the chef to have ready for serving at midnight. His skill must be applauded by all, in just a couple of hours he had to cook dinner for fifty-four men in an oven not much bigger that an ordinary domestic one. His working room was a little triangular space in the corner of the passage. Here he would have to cope with the pitching seas which sometimes would be tossing his utensils up and down like ping-pong balls.

The chief engineer held the rank of warrant officer, and his name was Stevens. He was very efficient and had the knack of being able to transmit his keen sense of duty to his subordinates. His pep talks to together with the guidance of the knowledgeable ERA Norris gave me such aspirations that I had soon become fully efficient with all operations in the after-ends. Towards the end of my first watch all four HP air reservoirs had been topped up to the required 4000 lbs per square inch pressure so I was more than happy to shut down both compressors. With both of these machines running in a confined space it was rather like sitting between two high-powered motorbikes at full throttle, the noise was deafening. Since joining the *Tetrarch* I had been given little or no time to get to know my new mess-mates. With this in mind I was more than pleased when I was relieved from my first watch. At last I would have the chance to join in the chatter with the remainder of the off-watch stokers within the mess.

The mess now had become a hive of activity. Seated on the bunk seats which surrounded two of the mess tables, half a dozen men were engaged in a losing battle while trying to hold down the dinner plates just long enough for another mess-mate to make an appetising presentation of roast turkey, roast potatoes, fresh greens and Yorkshire pudding. The broken remains of a few plates was evidence of the violent pitching and tossing which we were to endure for the next few days. Sitting by the third table, two of our leading stokers were busy serving out the rum ration. Seemingly untroubled by the violent movements of the boat, the dispensers held on to the white enamel jug. If the boat stood up on end there was no way that this dedicated rum bo'sun was going to spill so much as one molecule of this precious nectar. One by one each of us would join these two in order to scrutinise the full measure of our allotted tots, a rough sea would be no excuse for short measure. Although I write this with tongue in cheek, any wartime submariner would agree that our daily tot was a prize to be treasured during those long fearful patrols.

Having swallowed my tot, I set about the arduous task of eating my dinner. With one hand holding my plate in position I was left with no other option but to abandon my knife. Then using my fork in my right hand I was able to enjoy the excellent meal that the chef had cooked for us. In my quest to obtain advanced knowledge of expectations that lay before us, I asked my mess-mates to tell me about the previous patrol. There was no shortage of volunteers, they explained that each boat was assigned to cover a certain area which became known as a billet, or perhaps more accurately for chart purposes a grid. Every night the boat would advance to the next grid taking us further and further inside the Skaggerak. They went on to say that, as each boat advanced, the foremost boat would withdraw and gradually make its way back to the North Sea. For those who were fortunate enough to make the round trip, all that remained then, was to have a safe passage across the North Sea back to our home base in Rosyth.

While my thoughts dwelt on the information provided by my mess-mates and having listened to their account of the terrifying experience of being trapped and depth-charged for forty-two hours and at one time diving to a depth of six hundred feet, I was beginning to wish that I had never asked about it, especially when the buzz passed through the boat that we were about to repeat the same mission. Many times during the next two days, we were given good cause to crash dive. Threatened by the ever-increasing hostile aircraft, the surface was no place to flirt with such menaces. I may add that our own aircraft was no less hostile than that of the enemy. The practice of firing colour-coded recognition flares from the bridge often proved to be futile. Mistakes were made then, and continued to be made throughout the duration of the war.

During further conversation at dinner I learned that our captain, Lieutenant Commander Ronnie Mills was a fine captain who knew his stuff. I was also told that I had taken the place of a chap who had sprained his ankle earlier that day. Apart from the discomfort of being tossed about, the rest of the night passed without incident. When it was time to turn in I discovered that I had been given one of the most uncomfortable bunks in the mess. It was a top bunk and because of the contours of the boat's deck-head, I had to sleep with my knees almost tucked under my chin. At the head of the bunk a klaxon had been fitted to the bulkhead so when lying on my back I would get the full blast of the hooter in my ear. With every chance of this happening, it was not a comforting thought to sleep on. I had not long to wait before I suffered this painful experience. At about 1000 hours the next morning I was awakened with a start when I got the full blast of the klaxon in my left ear then as I shot up from my bunk I saw stars when I struck my forehead on the deck-head. From then on I always kept the klaxon stuffed up with a towel.

As we got near to the enemy coast, air attacks became more frequent but the ever-vigilant eyes of the sea-swamped lookouts gave us ample warning of the approaching menaces and so allowing us time to dive out of harm's way. At 0500 hours on the third day the captain ordered the crew to diving stations. Having penetrated the minefields guarding the entrance to the Skaggerak, he was preparing to set periscope watches while patrolling Norway's south-east coastline. Almost any schoolchild will confirm the fact that the geographical position of this part of the world produces the phenomenon of the aurora borealis. In order to keep our presence unknown it was necessary for us to remain submerged during those long twilight evenings. This precaution left us only three hours in which to charge our batteries. The routine of having to remain submerged for twenty-one hours a day became a welcome relief in many ways, at least we didn't have to suffer the discomfort caused by the rough seas above us. As well as being able to eat our meals in comfort we could pass our off-duty hours in more leisurely activities.

On that particular patrol I remember that a brand new game of monopoly was the prime source of amusement. This treasured possession together with an electric toaster had been presented to the *Tetrarch* by the good people in Barrow who had adopted us. After being submerged for some time a game was in progress when one of the stokers pushed aside the props and placed a large cooked ham on the end of the table.

'That looks tasty,' I said.

'Yes,' agreed Stoker Gilliam-Hill. 'That's for our wedges.'

'Wedges, what are they?' I queried.

Then in a jovial mood he replied, 'That is what some people call sandwiches.' He then went on to say, 'If you feel a bit peckish when you come off watch you can help yourself.'

A few hours later a couple of us decided to have a wedge but to our dismay all that remained of the joint was the bone. During the course of the day everyone in the mess was complaining that they hadn't so much as tasted the ham. 'Who the hell's had it?' they were asking. But no answer was forthcoming, and the incident remained a complete mystery.

At about 1000 hours the following day, the boat was dived and the whole of the stokers' mess was in darkness, save for a small pilot light glowing in the gangway. I was sitting on a box in the after-ends looking through a magazine. It so happened that I looked up from the book and peered into the shadows of the mess. My attention was drawn towards a movement in one of the top bunks. With upstretched arms one of the stokers was stealthily releasing the pin from a gas mask locker which was situated just above his head. After retrieving a thick ham sandwich he returned to the horizontal position scoffing away like a hungry wolf. That night when everybody was awake I told them that I had solved the mystery of the missing ham. Then, reaching out I opened up the hiding place and sure enough the evidence was staring us in the face. This prank left me no doubt in my mind, no matter what fate had in store for us, this guy at least was not going to die from starvation.

As the days slowly passed I found myself getting more and more disgruntled with the monotonous routine. Each day we would dive at 0400 hours and remained submerged in those ice-cold waters until midnight. At times it would get so cold that I would turn into my bunk wearing two sweaters. We had now been at sea for nearly two weeks and our only contact with the enemy was the distant rumbles of exploding depth-charges. Although I would suspect that by this time the captain would have been somewhat frustrated at having not made a killing, he would at least be consoled with the thought that for the time being the presence of our submarines had forced the enemy to keep all their ships within the sanctuary of their home ports. Towards the end of the patrol we had moved south into Danish waters and began to patrol the coast of Denmark.

One morning we came across a number of fishing vessels, each of which was flying a numbered pennant. It was suspected that these boats were being used to spot our positions and pass the information to the enemy. With this in mind the captain decided to investigate. It must have been quite a shock to their crew when we surfaced alongside one of them, having been at sea for more than two weeks with no prospect of getting a bigger prize, we had to leave our mark somewhere. At about 0800 hours, the captain ordered the third officer, ERA Trice, and two ratings to board the trawler. A few minutes later all except Trice returned to the submarine bringing with them the trawler's captain and his three crewmen. Trice was left with the job of scuttling the craft. Being close to the enemy shores prudence prevailed. No doubt our captain had reasoned that this method of sinking the boat was less noisy than a bang from a bloody great gun. Very soon Trice returned to the *Tetrarch* leaving the innocent-looking fishing vessel slowly sinking. After clearing the bridge the captain shut the conning tower hatch and our boat slid gently beneath the waves.

Later that day news had reached the after-ends that the trawler's captain and crew were chatting to some of our lads in the fore-ends. I then decided to go and hear what they had to say. On reaching the crew space I saw four dejected men sitting at the mess table. It was quite easy to deduce correctly that the man who was doing the talking was the captain. He was a fine looking man and had he been standing he would have towered head and shoulders above most of us present. His receding hairline gave way to a mass of golden locks. I estimated him to be about forty years old. With light blue eyes and weather-beaten cheeks he looked every bit a Danish seaman. Speaking fluent English he told us that he thought that we would lose the war. He said that he had seen large numbers of German tanks and that the overwhelming strength of their army would be too much for us to cope with. He then began to talk about his own plight. He told us that his life savings had gone into his boat and that his daughter was getting married later that day.

'In fact,' he said, 'we were just about to return to port when you surfaced alongside us.'

This part of his story was sad enough but there was worse to come. He said that they should have returned the day before but owing to their poor catch of fish they decided to spend an extra day at sea. Such are the fortunes of war! We remained in the area the whole of that day and much to Trice's embarrassment, the gunwales of the unfortunate captain's craft was still seen above the surface four hours later. Needless to say Trice became a victim of much leg-pulling which was graphically illustrated when Stoker Clulow, who was a gifted artist, pinned a comical sketch to the ship's noticeboard. It depicted the submarine's oversize gun trained at point blank range on a tiny fishing vessel, in the centre of which stood four fishermen with their hair sticking up on end with their hands raised towards the sky. Behind them a good likeness to Trixie Trice was knocking seven bells out of the bottom of the boat with a bloody big hammer.

That evening, news of the long-awaited signal delighted the heart of each man in the boat: we had been recalled to base. Even so we all realised that it was far too soon to start celebrating. Before we could even think about leave we knew that the long daytime surface run back to Rosyth would be fraught with danger. During the day's long dive, leaks from the HP air lines would be the cause of a gradual build up of air pressure within the hull. To avoid the captain making a hasty ascent through the conning tower hatch when surfacing, we had to risk breaking silent routine to run one of the air compressors until such time as the pressure within the boat had equalised with that of the outside atmosphere. While this operation was in progress the boat would be kept to a depth of thirty-two feet with the officer of the watchkeeping a vigilant lookout for enemy 'E' boats.

On this occasion the compressor had been running for about ten minutes when suddenly I became blinded by spraying water which seemed to swamp the whole compartment. Not knowing what had happened I screamed out for help. Within a few seconds ERA Norris came charging through, then leaning towards the back of the compressor he shut off the inlet and outlet valves to the machines water cooling system and to my relief the flow of the water stopped immediately. Turning towards Norris, I asked, 'What happened?'

'Nothing much to worry about, the boat has run into a fresh water patch, it often happens in these parts,' he replied. He then explained to me that in fresh water the boat had become less buoyant and had suddenly plunged to a depth greater than the circulating system on the compressors could withstand. To allow for such an eventuality a copper disc was fitted to each compressor and what had happened was that the extra pressure created by the sudden change of depth caused the safety disc to explode. Although the hole was only three-quarters of an inch in diameter the force was so great that the blinding spray swamped the whole compartment. It was a lesson that I would never forget.

Apart from the fact that the German 'E' boats caused us to take evasive action from time to time, our trip home proved to be uneventful. As we berthed alongside the quay at Rosyth an armed escort was waiting on the jetty. Our captain was furious and looking towards them he shouted, 'What the devil do you want?'

'We have come for the prisoners, sir,' retorted the officer in charge of the escort.

'You go back to where you came from, these are not prisoners they are guests.'

Then, with a flea in his ear, the officer ordered his squad to turn tail and hastened away from the quayside. In the meantime I had removed the dog-clips and opened the after hatch and within a few seconds us stokers were standing on the after casing taking our first breath of fresh air for eighteen days. Those of us who were off duty hurried to collect our cooking and eating utensils, all of which had to be transferred to the parent ship which was moored up in the basin about half a mile away.

Father Time is not my only excuse for my memories of that night's orgy being a little obscure, after all I was now a blooded submariner and had every right to join forces with half a dozen of the *Tetrarch* stokers in celebrating my return from my first patrol in a submarine. One thing that I do remember about that night, was the meeting up with some of the crew of the Polish submarine *Orzel*. Having made a daring escape from Nazi occupied Poland they continued fighting the war operating from Rosyth. The few of the crew that we shared the night's fun with were a friendly bunch of lads, but alas our friendship was only to last for a few hours. The *Orzel* and its fine crew were destined for doom when it left Rosyth to go on their next patrol on the following morning. Soon after returning to the parent ship the next morning I was to learn of other losses among our submarines. These losses had claimed three more of my classmates in Fort Blockhouse, in less that two months only three out of eight of us survived. After dinner the effect of my daily rum ration gave me the urge to make my way across the dockyard towards the wet canteen. There I joined company with others of our crew who were already in the mood to continue celebrations. After downing a few pints and sharing in their bravado, I was able to put all thoughts of depression behind me. I had already decided long before, that no matter what fate had in store for me, these were the lads I would want to be with.

Much to my displeasure, destiny had other ideas as regards my future inasmuch as a few days later Chief Stoker Pearson poked his head into the after-ends saying, 'Shats, you are on draft back to the spare crew.'

'Why?' I asked.

He then told me that I had only come to the boat on a temporary basis and the other stoker that I replaced was now out of hospital and back in the boat. A few encouraging remarks did little to dispel my disappointment, then after being told that I would be recommended as a promising candidate for a future in submarines I packed my belongings and left the boat. On my papers today there is no record of me ever doing that patrol, but bearing in mind that I did get a last minute draft I am not surprised. I would not be the last one to get what was to become known as a 'pier-head jump'. I have no doubt that such slap-happy regulating in the drafting office was the cause of a lot of confusion regards who was where, when a boat was lost on patrol.

Only a few days had passed when at midnight Leading Stoker Tim Healy, myself and one other stoker whose name I never knew, had a rude awakening. 'Pack your bags at once you are to catch the next train to Dundee. From there you will join the mine-laying submarine *Thames*.'

As far as I was concerned this to me was bad news. I had once seen this old boat in dry dock and I thought that it was far too big and clumsy to compete against the air attacks such as I had so recently experienced. Our night-time train journey took us over a long curved iron structure which Tim told us was the Tay bridge. As if I didn't have enough to worry about, while crossing it, Tim gave me an explicit account of the train that toppled over the side of it many years before. We arrived at the quayside where the *Thames* was tied up just before daybreak. I can vividly remember standing at the end of the gangway in the chill of the morning. We were met by a chief PO who was most likely the *Thames*'s coxswain. 'We now only require one stoker because the other two men are no longer adrift.' Then looking at me and the other stoker he said, 'You two had better toss for it.'

From that moment on, I have engraved in my mind the sad memories of spinning that coin. At the time I had no way of knowing that my life depended on the correct call, because that patrol was the *Thames*'s last. As for myself it was the beginning of a charmed life. Soon after we arrived back on the *Forth* Tim told me that he had received a letter from Dundee saying that the *Thames* had been sunk by a Sunderland flying boat when on anti-submarine patrol. I still have no reason to disbelieve that there was more than an element of truth in this strong rumour regards the fate of the *Thames* which at that time seemed to be common knowledge among the *Forth*'s spare crew. It was said that the crew of the Sunderland had taken photos as the *Thames* took its last dive. The official records now state that it was probably sunk by a mine off Norway. Here I am reminded of the old adage: the first casualty of war is the truth.

Chapter Four

Flying High

The splendid food and comfortable surroundings provided by the spare crew mess was all too good to last. With this in mind I began to exploit all available leave and enjoy the good things in life for as long as I could. So a month's pay in my pocket provided me with enough wealth to spend a full week on a bender. Having spent my last night on a final fling in Edinburgh I was now on my way back to the ship. As I approached the Rosyth dockyard gates I saw the lone figure of a sailor walking towards me. Although the distance between us was too great for facial recognition I immediately became aware of the all too familiar jaunty gait of a very dear chum whom I first befriended during those hectic days of square bashing, which was followed by a continuing friendship on our first ship together. As we drew closer together the broad grin on his face fully expressed the joy of the reunion, which was of course mutual.

As we shook hands, I said 'Hello Chippy, how are you and where are you off to at this time of the day?'

He then told me that his ship had docked and he had been given twenty-four hours' leave.

I answered by saying, 'That is tough because I am due back on board at 0900 so I have not much time now, but I shall see you tomorrow.'

'I am afraid not because our ship has been badly damaged and I am being drafted back to Chatham tomorrow morning,' he answered.

It was then on a sudden impulse and all out of character that I replied, 'Sod the consequences, I am staying ashore with you,' and so we turned away from the dockyard gates and made our way towards the Rosyth to Inverkeithing ferry boat. Over several pints of beer the two of us exchanged our war experiences and after listening to him describing how his ship was repeatedly bombed during a run up the east coast I began to realise that my lot in submarines was not so bad after all, at least if we survived the initial attack from a bomber we could always dive the boat and get out of harm's way. During further conversation Chippy told me that he too had thoughts about volunteering for service in submarines. He then asked me what I thought about them. My reply to his question was one of encouragement. I explained that although I had only been in subs a couple of months I was already hooked on the comradeship of my fellow crew-mates. That to me was always something special. Being fully convinced that we would soon be seeing one another again Chippy and I parted company at 0800 the following morning. I then boarded the parent ship HMS *Forth* to face the music knowing full well that it would be my commanding officer that would be calling the tune. Offering no excuse for being twenty-four hours adrift I was duly awarded fourteen days stoppage of leave and pay, together with fourteen days number elevens. During the first few days of my punishment I was drafted to the submarine *Triad* where my punishment was to continue until we put to sea ten days later.

My record was not the kind of legacy that my superiors would welcome and I soon became aware that the chief and POs did not want a leave-breaker in the crew. As for the coxswain, he made quite sure that I would suffer my penance to the bitter end. The *Triad* at that time was berthed about a quarter of a mile away from the parent ship. Each morning both seamen and stokers would muster on the quayside and from there coxswain would take command and march us down to the boat. One morning I was about to join the ranks when he pounced on me for not wearing a ribbon on my cap. I tried to explain that I was employed on a dirty job in the engine room but I should have saved my breath. He made it quite clear to all that he was after my blood. After giving me a stiff dressing-down I joined the ranks along with my fellow stokers and we were marched away. As I looked around I could see at least three others without cap ribbons and not a word was said to them.

This was also noticed by Stoker Rigby who said in a loud voice, 'None of us are wearing cap ribbons, why the hell don't they leave him alone? They are always having a go at him.'

Soon after, I welcomed the news that we were about to put to sea again, not that I particularly relished another patrol in the Skaggerak, the fact was that I knew that the first turn of the screws would put an end to my punishment musters.

The same evening after slipping our moorings we were heading towards May Island, and as I expected en route towards Norway. Much to my disgust I was given the job of ERA's mess-man. This meant as well as keeping watch in the engine room I had to prepare and serve their meals three times a day, so what with peeling spuds, washing dishes and acting as a general flunky, I soon became completely exhausted through the lack of sleep. At dinner times the chief ERA always seemed to find something to do in the engine room and so required individual service which stopped me from getting my proper rest. This annoyed me so much that one day when he went off leaving his dinner on the table I ditched it in the gash bucket. I then washed up the dishes, cleaned up the mess and went back to my bunk. About half an hour later he sent for me and asked what I had done with his dinner. When I told him I thought he didn't want it and so I ditched it, for some strange reason he hit the roof. My action credited me with a black mark but it put an end to the chief's dinner-time walkabout.

As far as I can remember our voyage towards the Skaggerak was uneventful except perhaps for a few crash dives which at that time had become part and parcel of our daily routine. The next few days we spent patrolling off the coast of Norway but despite the captain's unrelenting efforts to make contact with the enemy, no such engagement was forthcoming. There was however one particular day that I shall never forget. I was lying in my bunk when I became aware of distant depth-charging. The sound of explosions seemed to last for hours as we ourselves grew closer to where it was all happening. Feeling restless I moved from my bunk and made my way towards the control room. There in the dim lighting I studied the grim faces of the watchkeepers and as I looked towards the chart table the captain was diligently surveying the charts, indeed the whole atmosphere seemed extremely tense.

Breaking the dead silence I whispered to one of my colleagues, 'Some poor devil's going through it.'

'Yes,' he agreed, 'it's the *Shark*. They are taking a real hammering.' Although we ourselves were a mile away from the scene of violence, the severity of the attack was almost unbearable to witness. I think we all guessed that the *Shark* would not survive the onslaught. To our sorrow she was confirmed lost soon afterwards. It wasn't until many years after I learned that although the boat itself was lost, there was quite a number of survivors who were taken prisoners of war.

It was now eighteen days since we left Rosyth and after being recalled to base we set course for home. The passage across the North Sea was to be one of the most gruesome surface runs that I would ever experience during seven years of wartime in submarines. I lost count of the number of times attacking aircraft forced us to crash dive and with each dive the bombs came closer and closer. During one of my watches in the engine room we were forced down three times within half an hour, each time the bombs exploded as we reached the depth of fifty feet or so.

It was during one of those dives that the ERA stopped the engines while I leapt on to the small footplate and was rapidly shutting down the starboard muffler valve, when with one blinding flash my head seemed to burst open as a gigantic explosion directly above my head blew me sprawling across the engine room footplates. This gave my skull a cracking blow against the port engine leaving me half-dazed with a half inch cut in my bonce glaring up at the hull expecting the whole lot to cave in at any moment. By the time I came to my senses the boat had rapidly reached a depth of eighty feet and the chief ERA had noticed that the engine cooling water gauge was registering well over the maximum safety pressure. As he moved towards me I realised that I had not completely shut the muffler valve and so allowed the sea water to find its way back to the engine. The incident was regarded as negligence on my part and considering the circumstances I thought it to be most unfair. Consequently the engineer put me on captain's report.

By now I was feeling very low, the passage home had been frightening enough, and the thought of having to face the captain only added to my misery. Soon after entering harbour I was told that either myself or one other particular stoker would be granted five days' leave. The usual practice at that time was if one had completed two patrols he would be granted this leave but according to the records neither of us had qualified so it was decided that we should draw out of the hat. I then explained to the chief stoker that I had done two patrols one of which was on the *Tetrarch* just prior to joining the *Triad*. I said it was probably not recorded because I got a pier-head jump to it. However, much to my annoyance the chief stoker was in no mood to investigate my claim.

'I am sorry but you will still have to draw for it,' he said.

Soon afterwards I was summoned to the control room to take part in the draw. Then for the first time since I joined the *Triad* things seemed to go right for me; I won the draw. Unfortunately half an hour later the chief stoker came to my mess and told me that the draw would no longer stand. Then offering me no explanation as to why he overruled the result of the draw he told my opposite number that he could go in my place. I could only sense that favouritism had settled the issue. Then to add insult to injury the coxswain sent for me, only to tell me to change into the rig of the day and prepare myself to take the afternoon watch as trot sentry.

By twelve noon the whole crew had departed from the boat leaving me to complete a four hour watch on the casing. After being supplied with belt and gaiters together with a service revolver I began to pace up and down the casing. Having little knowledge of seamanship and being completely unaware of moving tides, I assumed that my only job was to shoot any would be fifth column saboteur that may have popped up from behind one of the wooden crates which were standing on the jetty. Fortunately my reaction to such an encounter was never to be tested, instead I found myself becoming very bored. By mid-afternoon my thoughts wandered toward the dockyard canteen where I could visualise all my mess-mates enjoying a good old booze-up. In the meantime I had to suffer the agony until I was relieved from duty at 1600 hours. Although my relief was a well-seasoned able bodied seaman and well acquainted with the rise and fall of the tide, he had no chance to grasp the fact that the boat was hanging high and dry, that is to say not before I was well out of hailing distance. My speedy departure was made possible through the courtesy of one of the *Triad*'s officers who had been kind enough to leave his peddle cycle behind one of the wood crates on the jetty. I had seen it there all day so I thought no harm would be done if I borrowed it for a little while. It turned out that I had made a bad guess when I decided that he would not want to use it again that day. Unknown to me he and his wife lived locally and while she was waiting anxiously for him to come home for tea he was rushing around the dockyard like a raving lunatic trying to discover where some idiot had left his bike. If he had only looked near to the entrance to the canteen he would have found it much sooner, because that is where I had left it in my hurry to get a beer.

As I entered the crowded bar a roaring cheer dominated the general rowdiness of light-hearted sailors letting off steam. As I looked in the direction of the cheering, the welcoming gestures of a dozen sailors beckoned me over towards their table. I recognised them to be some of the crew from the light cruiser. HMS *Dragon* which had been my last ship in general service. A few steps towards their table was to burden me with more trouble. After handshakes all round an extra chair was pulled up to the table inviting me to join in the orgy. Having accepted the invitation my priority was to get on level terms with my already inebriated colleagues so I wasted no time in downing a few pints. Now that I was in submarines they seemed to regard me as some sort of hero or lunatic, I wasn't sure which. However I must confess I did enjoy the limelight and offered little or no resistance to the continual flow of free beer. These celebrations lasted for two hours. The party then dispersed leaving me the task of finding my way back to the parent ship.

When I entered the *Triad*'s mess I discovered that it was devoid of all personnel.

'Where are they?' I shouted to the neighbouring boat's crew.'

'They have all been called back to the boat, they have been there since just after 1600 hours, the afternoon watchkeeper forgot to ease out the tie-ropes and springs with the falling tide so the boat was left hanging eighteen foot out of the water.'

'Bloody hell, that was me. Now I'm for it,' I said. Judging by the snide remarks that I received from all quarters it seemed that every one had shown a keen interest in the matter. Looking back over the years, dare I say that the submarine *Triad* was the first recorded UFO sighted over Britain. At 0900 the next morning I was taken before my captain who in no uncertain terms left me in no doubt that he was not amused by my irresponsible deeds. The severity of the charges left him no alternative, he was obliged to forward the case to Captain 'S'. Two or three days had lapsed before I was finally summoned to appear on HMS *Forth*'s quarterdeck for Captain 'S's defaulters. Although my mess-mates were not entirely unsympathetic towards me, I had already decided to offer no excuse for my behaviour and that I would accept the punishment without complaining.

Earlier that morning I had been drawn into a heated argument. I was sitting in the mess when I was approached by the stoker who I had replaced on the *Triad* a month earlier.

'I hear you are in a spot of trouble,' he said.

'That must be the understatement of the year,' I answered. I then tried to explain that I thought I had been victimised from the first moment that I stepped aboard. I then said, 'As far as I am concerned the sooner I see the back of the *Triad* the better.'

This man immediately responded with a verbal attack. He implied that I had deliberately antagonised certain individuals in order to get off the boat.

'I think you are yellow,' he scorned. His remark shook me rigid. Although at no time during my exploits did I regard myself as a hero I certainly was not a coward. After all, the war at that time was only six months old, four of which I had spent patrolling the North Atlantic. I thought that was a good record by any standards. Allowing for the fact that this man did not know me I swallowed the bitter pill and did nothing to retaliate.

At 0900 the next day HMS *Forth*'s tannoy blurted out the order, 'Captain "S"'s defaulters muster outside the regulating office.'

I was soon to discover that I was not the only one to have butterflies in his stomach. There were at least three others all of whom were on lesser charges than I. After comparing our misdemeanours I was quite sure that I was the one who had most to worry about. As soon as the master-at-arms arrived on the scene I was ordered to stand at attention and then marched towards a high desk which had been placed in the centre of the quarterdeck. I was then ordered to halt at one pace in front of it, then having obeyed the age old order, 'Off cap.' I stood motionless while Captain 'S' listened inattentively to my accuser who stated that on two occasions I had exposed the *Triad* to danger by failing to execute my duties in the proper manner.

For a few agonising seconds I stood in silence while the Captain studied my service records. He paused for a moment then turning towards the *Triad*'s engineer officer he asked him if he could be more explicit in his condemnation of my behaviour. Had I hoped that both he and the chief ERA had relented in their harsh judgement on me I would have been doomed to disappointment. They were both very hostile towards me. They told Captain 'S' that I was most unsuitable for service in submarines and recommended that I should be drafted back to general service. I knew that I would be punished but not in this way.

However Captain 'S' had other ideas. Leaning towards me from the other side of the desk, he looked me straight in the eye and asked, 'Have you anything you wish to say?'

I immediately seized the opportunity to make a last ditch attempt to rescue my ego which by now had been shattered. In an instant I decided to reverse my former decision and tell of the unfair harassment which I had endured over the last month or so. In desperation I left nothing uncovered. I concluded my plea by telling him that the engineer officer of the *Tetrarch* had given me an excellent reference regarding my future in submarines. I then asked if he could speak on my behalf.

Turning towards the officer of the watch, Captain 'S' asked if the *Tetrarch* was still alongside. After receiving an affirmative reply he ordered the messenger to tell the *Tetrarch* engineer officer that his presence was required on the quarterdeck. Within a few minutes the messenger returned with Warrant Officer Stevens at his heels who, not knowing what was going on, looked somewhat puzzled.

When questioned Stevens eagerly supported my claim to a good reference and when asked if he would have me back on board the *Tetrarch* he replied, 'Yes anytime.'

Captain 'S' then turned to me and said, 'Case dismissed. You are drafted to the *Tetrarch* from p.m. today.'

Chapter Five

Into the Arena

Within minutes I was presenting myself to a man who in peacetime would have been counting his days before retiring on his Naval pension, but like so many other good men who had served their twenty-two years, would never draw it. His name was Geordie Pearson, the chief stoker of the *Tetrarch*. He was a fine fatherly figure of a man, a character that I would have been proud to emulate.

'Well, I am here to stay this time, chief,' I said to him.

'Sorry about your trouble, behave yourself and you can put all that behind you,' he answered. He went on to say that he would put me on the duty roster and I would be given back my old job in the after-ends. The man that I had called upon to pull me out of the stew that morning kept his word, he said that a flunky's job afforded very little scope for an untrained stoker to gain experience in a submarine. I could only regard the qualities of this man with high esteem. It was not only that he stood by his first assessment of my abilities, he was also a very capable officer regarding his own knowledge of the boat. On my first patrol I had observed that his know-how did not stop within the boundaries of the engine room bulkhead, he was equally at home in the fore-ends, after-ends or the control room. On patrol off Norway I had seen him keep periscope watches with inspiring efficiency. I venture to say that this was unique because I never witnessed any other engineer who did so throughout my ten years in submarines. With impressive fervour for efficiency he had a knack of imparting his knowledge and so giving us young and inexperienced stokers a will to learn.

As for my part in this schooling, I was put to work under the guidance of a twenty-three year old ERA. He answered to the name of Norris. As I write, the ghost of this man remains vivid in my memory. He was just under six foot tall with a fine-looking face which was dominated by locks of dark brown curly hair hanging over his brow. Altogether his good looks and pleasant manner matched the efficient and explicit way he was able to teach me to operate the HP air compressors, also the alternative methods of operating the steering and hydroplane machinery. My former messmates had given me a hearty welcome on my return to the *Tetrarch* and most of them had learned of my unhappy experience on the *Triad*. If any of them thought that my plight was self inflicted none of them showed it.

A comment made by Stoker Gilliam-Hill described in full the way that I was received by all. 'You will be all right with us Shats, the buzz is that we are going out to the Med.'

This was confirmed later that morning when the sound of the coxswain's voice echoed over the boat's tannoy. 'All ship's company muster in the fore-ends.'

'This is it, the Med for sure,' somebody said.

After we assembled, our captain, Lieutenant-Commander Ronnie Mills, edged his way to the front of the crowd and climbed a few rungs up the fore-end ladder, then turning round to face us he ordered, 'Ship's company at ease.' Then pausing for a few seconds he said, 'I have got you here together to inform you that we have now been assigned to enter the arena of combat and very soon we shall be patrolling the Mediterranean Sea where our pickings will be more plentiful than of late.'

As he spoke I felt sure that I was not alone when my

thoughts turned towards my loved ones at home. The disaster of Dunkirk was but a month old and the possibilities of a German invasion could not be dismissed from my mind and here I was being sent further afield. As if sensing our innermost thoughts our captain tried to console us by reminding us that we would be a lot more comfortable patrolling under the Mediterranean sun than it had been in the Arctic conditions of the Norwegian fjords.

He went on to say, 'Now is the good news, in a couple of days we shall be docking at Tyneside and each watch will be given seven days' leave.'

Then in the midst of loud cheers our captain withdrew from the fore-ends seemingly convinced with the firm knowledge that he had managed to boost the crew's morale despite the unwelcome news that we were being sent overseas. As the crew dispersed I became aware of the usual mutterings and comments in the background.

'Is he stone deaf? Didn't he hear the hundred and five depth-charges that the Germans dropped on us while we were up the fjords? If that is not the arena of combat, what is?' someone grumbled.

Within a couple of days our boat was rounding May Island and heading south. During the forenoon the next day, the *Tetrarch* came to rest in the centre of Swan-Hunters dry dock at Wallsend. Seconds after the order, 'Fall out harbour stations,' the men allocated for first leave piled into the mess like swarming bees. After diving into their lockers the mess was in a turmoil with suits and clobber flying about all over the place. It looked more like a church hall jumble sale than a submarine mess-deck. Meanwhile those of us who were to remain on board were put to work removing the barnacles from the hull and all fittings beneath the boat's waterline. Many months had passed since the boat's hull had seen the light of day so the build up of crustaceans would by now be the cause of a certain amount of drag thereby reducing the boat's speed. The closing of the lock gates was the signal to start pumping out the dock. Suspended from lines secured to the casing were half a dozen rafts. Each of these was manned by one seaman equipped with a long-handled broom and a scraper. As the water level inched its way down the hull, these seamen were scrubbing away as fast as they could.

As I watched I asked one of them, 'What's all the rush about?'

He explained to me that this operation had to be done while the hull was still wet. Once dry, he said it would be almost impossible to remove the barnacles. This was a fact which I was to discover for myself an hour or so later. When the dock was dry, along with two other stokers I was given the job of removing the barnacles from the boat's screws. Working from a stage supported by tall trestles we scraped and polished for a couple of days or more until eventually the job was completed to Warrant Officer Steven's satisfaction.

With half the boat's crew now on leave, the twenty-four of us that remained behind were split into two watches so that every other night we were able to partake in what came to be known as screamers, appropriately named by Stoker Bell after he and a few others had returned to the boat screaming mad with drink. For obvious reasons it became necessary for the crew to be victualled ashore. This arrangement caused a great deal of discontentment among the crew. The building in which we were victualled was less than third rate, it was in fact a rest home for vagrants. A few of the lads sarcastically called it 'Simpsons Hotel'. If the name meant something to the upmarket hoteliers nobody had told me about it. I really took it as gospel, as far as I was concerned we were staying at 'Simpsons Hotel'.

Two years later I was trying to describe the place to one of the ERA's aboard the *Thrasher*, he told me that the only building that exists in that part of Wallsend was a tramps' doss-house. 'I should know because I live quite near to it,' he told me. However in spite of our moans and groans nothing was done to alter the situation, and as always Jolly Jack had the perfect logical explanation which was frequently expressed over each meal. 'Somebody is making a pay day out of this.' In such circumstances this time-honoured phrase has become as immortal to the Navy as Nelson's 'England expects'.

The preparation for our stint in the Med kept us very busy and in no time at all it was our turn to go on leave. Then as one might expect the week's leave had soon become a passing memory. Although people were very aware of the war at sea, there was little else happening in London to indicate that the country was at war. Apart from seeing so many people in uniform, everything else seemed the same. There was one occasion when I observed a German reconnaissance plane high above the Thames, but this I thought was no immediate threat.

With all leave over it was now 3rd September, 1940. For some reason that September date was becoming a habitual red letter day in my lifetime. To begin with it was 3rd September, 1937, while aboard the *Arethusa* that I was ploughing my way through the English Channel on my way to the Mediterranean to begin my first commission overseas. Then, 3rd September, 1939, I was ploughing through the same channel (that time I was aboard the light cruiser *Dragon*) and our ship was heading north for Scapa Flow. Yet again it was 3rd September, 1940, and I was once again bound for the Mediterranean, but this time I was in a submarine. The whole trip from Tyneside down the North Sea, round the Straits of Dover, through the English Channel and through the Bay of Biscay was completed on the surface. To my amazement it happened without incident.

As I have already explained the North Sea and English Channel were hotbeds of terror at that time, what with German 'E' boats and even more menacing our own, as well as German air patrols, all of which were hostile opponents to any submarine. Although we could always recognise our own aircraft, we could not rely on them to read our colour-coded flares correctly. Only three months earlier I had endured such attacks while returning from patrol aboard the *Triad*. Without a doubt it was foul weather that spared us from these menaces. The violence of the pitching and tossing became a real challenge for us, it was barely the beginning of our voyage yet already our eating utensils had been reduced to four plates and a couple of mugs. Some of the losses were unavoidable but quite a lot of it was due to carelessness. Often at mealtimes more food finished up on the deck than was eaten.

Now and again I would take a walk along to the fore-ends to stretch my legs and at the same time try to find out the latest news that may have been passed along the grapevine. As I passed through the control room I encountered a huge canvas bath which had been rigged up beneath the conning tower ladder. Although the helmsman was skilfully keeping the boat's bows into the oncoming seas every now and again he would get it wrong. Any such error of judgement would be instantly punished by the elements. The dynamic forces of the mountainous waves would pound over the hull broadside on. Then like a shot from a gun the whole steel hull would be tossed like a feather in the boiling seas. Then having aired her screws the gallant lady would send them crashing to the ocean as she would once again try to regain her equilibrium. She would then keel over and respond with an agonising shudder which would shake her from bow to stern. Full seas which periodically swamped the bridge and its occupants would pour down through the conning tower filling the canvas bath to the brim. To keep the bath dry it was necessary to employ an extra hand working full time on the job. A portable hose was rigged from the ballast pump ring main to the bottom of the bath so that each time it was flooded by the sea, the water could be sucked away by the ballast pump. As both main engines hungrily gulped at the night air, it was creating a cold damp draught much to the discomfort of the control room watchkeepers. Supporting myself by grasping at various fittings I warily made my way forward towards the seamen's mess. With each step I took I was navigating my way through overhanging sea-soaked Ursular suits and other garments which had temporary been discarded by the off duty lookouts. Any hope they may have had of getting them dry for their next duty would surely be a pipe dream. Often when I had seen them climbing back into those cold wet suits I had thanked my lucky stars that I was a stoker. Peering through the curtains into the seamen's mess I could see the figures of five men already garbed in their sea clothing, with their eyes covered with dark glasses, they sat in a crouched position beneath a couple of occupied bunks. With their mess in semi-darkness these bespectacled seamen were preparing to take over the next watch. This exercise was brought about by the necessity for the lookouts visual senses to be fully alert and adjusted for night vision from the first moment they stepped on to the bridge. Without diligent lookout's a submarine's life would be very short indeed.

The rough seas persisted throughout the voyage. Although most of us by then had regained our sea legs, there still remained a few that had not. One evening after we had dispensed the rum ration one of my mess-mates who had been lying on his bunk was seized with a sudden bout of sea-sickness. Being unable to reach the gash bucket in time, to my annoyance he picked up the lid of the mess fanny into which he vomited. He then staggered into the after-ends and poured its contents into a gash bucket. Realising that this utensil would soon be required for collecting the dinner from the galley, I looked on with some concern. For some reason or other my attention to the matter was momentary distracted, but it was long enough for a third party to have made a return trip to the galley. I was horrified when I saw him holding the unwashed lid filled to the brim with my favourite vegetable – cabbage. While the dinner was being distributed on the few remaining plates, I decided to keep quiet about it and just reject my own ration of cabbage. My silence lasted just long enough for all to devour their meal, by which time I could no longer resist the temptation, I had to tell them. While some of my messmates responded with a whole host of accusations leaving me in doubt of my birthright, others with weaker constitutions had become preoccupied by taking part in a marathon towards the gash bucket.

About a week had passed since we left Tyneside. Although the BBC news bulletin reported ever-increasing air raids on London, the morale of the crew was still very high but nevertheless I could not help thinking that we were pursuing the fight in the wrong direction. I would have been much happier if we had been allowed to continue the battle in home waters and for a brief spell I thought that I would get the chance to do just that. One afternoon the dreary routine was interrupted when the order, 'Diving stations,' was blurted out over the tannoy. As usual the buzz was soon passed to us in the after-ends. Our informant told us that smoke had been seen on the horizon and that we had been shadowing a ship for some time. It seemed that the captain was diving the boat so that he could close in and get a better sight of the possible prey. We were at the time near to the neutral port of Lisbon so the captain had to be certain that the ship was a legitimate target. The sinking of a neutral ship would have caused an international incident with disastrous consequences for our captain. Hence his decision to dive the boat in order to make an unobserved close up inspection. The outcome of his inspection was brought to a climax when he asked one of his officers to select a boarding party. Thinking that there was a good chance of taking the ship back to the UK I instantly volunteered, but was rejected in favour of a bigger man. With the gun's crew standing by for action we broke surface. After the boarding party had exchanged dialogue with the freighter's captain it was decided to escort the ship into the port of Lisbon. Being satisfied that the freighter together with its cargo was out of reach of the enemy, the neutrality laws forced us to up anchor the next morning and continue our voyage to Gibraltar.

This haven of peace and tranquillity was still a day or so away and already our food ration had been reduced to a monotonous diet of tinned food and ship's biscuits. The luxury of biting through a new crusty loaf of bread was more than a week behind us. Regarding the making of bread, the very nature of a submarine's environment made this task a tedious one and success would depend on a great deal of ingenuity and improvisation. Due to the sudden expansion of the submarine service, experienced cooks had become almost as extinct as the dodo and the green-horns of the day had a lot to learn. The build-up of the cold damp air pressure within the hull would create havoc with the normal tendency of the mixture of flour, yeast and water to rise. More often than not the bread was so hard that it was impossible to chew it. Having survived the cook's earlier endeavours, I couldn't help thinking that his war effort as a cook was wasted. If his talent had been directed towards building bomb-proof air-raid shelters, he would have achieved a greater service for his country. But to be fair, every submariner would agree that a cook's job in a submarine is the most demanding occupation in the boat.

One evening when we were feeling a bit peckish, Joe Grisdale and myself were sorting out some tinned food which we kept in a spare locker.

'Have you ever tasted hobo soup?' Joe asked.

'What the hell is that?' I answered.

'You go and muster up some bread and I will show you,' he said.

My mission took me scavenging in every nook and cranny in the seamen's mess and fore-ends where I managed to acquire what could just about be recognised as two loaves of bread, one of which I took from a gash bucket.

'Are you going to eat that?' one of the seamen asked.

'It's better than ours back aft,' I replied.

Then as I hastened away he shouted, 'You stokers must have cast iron guts.'

As I entered the stokers' mess I placed my prize possession on the table. As Joe began to mix together the vile concoction of soup, herrings in tomato, a tin of sardines and for good measure a tin of marmalade, I set about the task of cleaning up the bread. First of all I cut away the outside crust which was completely covered with mildew, I then cut the loaves into slices which revealed veins of green mould running in all directions so that they looked like small slabs of marble or road maps. After an excellent job of surgery I managed to salvage a couple of handfuls of diced bread which I promptly added to our splendid cuisine, and then stirred into this inspired creation no less than a tablespoon of black pepper. We then placed it on a hotplate and brought the whole lot to the boil. Much to my astonishment only Joe and I would eat the stuff. As we both scoffed away great beads of sweat poured from our brows while we complimented each other on its delicious taste. To be truthful the bloody stuff was burning our throats out but neither of us would give in. Under the watchful eyes of our mess-mates we took up the challenge to eat it all while we tried to convince each other how much we were enjoying it. Although we were not exactly on the borders of starvation, such bravado as this did cause laughter and so help to while away the time.

Soon after, we entered Gibraltar harbour and tied up alongside the mole. We had not been there long before most of us took advantage of a beautiful sunny day and went for a dip off the stern of the boat. A light-hearted feeling which at the time existed in the boat's crew was soon to become marred by the depressing news from home. The Battle of Britain was at its height and for the first time we realised that our loved ones at home were more exposed to danger than ourselves.

Now that we were in port one of my first requirements was a much needed haircut. The necessity for me to take drastic measures so as to rid myself of the offending growth, was brought home to me when I was put to work beneath the bilge plates where dripping oil from above soaked my hair. My long fringe had been annoying me by repeatedly falling into my eyes and so blurring my vision. As soon as the job was done I was on my way to find a barber. Wearing only a pair of football shorts and sandals I wandered across the gangplank and along the jetty. My quest took me towards a bell tent which accommodated a lone barber who was already poised to make a violent attack on my brown locks.

'How would you like it cut?' he enquired.

'Take the lot off,' I replied.

'Do you mean that you want me to shave it?' he queried.

'That's right. I have had enough of it, my hair keeps flopping into my eyes and blinding me.'

With a shrug of his shoulders he reluctantly hacked away at my hair before shaving my skull clean. Feeling as naked as a plucked turkey I was very soon walking back to the boat and I chuckled to myself as I wondered what kind of a reception that I would get from my crew-mates. As I drew level with the fore-hatch, to my horror both the captain and the first lieutenant stepped on to the casing. Having nowhere to hide I stood to one side to let them pass then after taking a few steps they turned to look back in my direction, and at the same time speak to the sentry. Not being able to hear what was said I waited for them to disappear and walked back towards the sentry who by now was doubled up with laughter.

'The captain has just asked me if you were one of his crew and when the Jimmy took a second look at you, he said, "It looks like Stoker Shattock." "Good heavens he looks like a bloody pirate," said the captain.'

The following afternoon I was looking over a new toy that had recently been issued to the boat, namely a rubber foldboat. It had been assembled that morning so that a couple of officers could try it out. Looking at it with some interest I asked if I could have a go. The coxswain said I could but I would have to get permission from the duty officer. After doing so, one of the ABs and myself carefully stepped into the boat and went paddling off towards the centre of the harbour. The expected afternoon's fun very soon came near to disaster. We had paddled about half a mile from the boat when the silly sod with me decided to stand up in the boat and wave to the lads who were stand-ing on the casing. The next thing I know we were both in the drink with the foldboat upside down and all its paddles and seats being carried away by the current, while the AB kept disappearing beneath the water frantically waving his arms screaming out for me to save him.

'I can't swim,' he was shouting.

'What a bloody time to tell me that,' I screamed back at him.

With my crew-mate about to take up residence with Davy Jones I was faced with the task of keeping his head above water and righting the boat at the same time. I don't know how, but I managed to do both. I was then able to calm him down and persuade him to hang on to the stern of the foldboat while I swam all over the ocean to rescue the bits and pieces which were by now halfway to Malta. Eventually when I did manage to get everything back into the boat, I had to think about getting back to the shore.

Realising that the boat was too unstable for my panic stricken crew-mate to climb into it, I told him to hang on while I swam with my legs pushing the craft by its stern. I had been to Gibraltar a few times before but until that day I did not realise that the harbour was so big, and by the time I had reached the nearest landing point I was completely shattered. Having helped my accomplice up the steep rocks of the mole he was in such a state of shock that he was unable to give me any help while I struggled up the rocks with the boat. However I did manage to drag it up on my own and apart from a few scratches on its bottom the boat was none the worse after our escapade.

To satisfy the mood of a certain few it seemed that no run ashore would be complete without a swim, so each night when returning to the boat we would dive into the harbour fully clothed. We had been in port about three days when one of the stokers looked into the escape chamber and saw a pile of white suits soaked in crude oil.

'Some of you had a good run ashore last night,' he said.

'You should come with us sometime,' answered Grisdale.

The stoker took another look at the ruined clothes, 'Much too expensive,' he remarked.

'Oh no,' replied Grisdale, 'you don't need much money but you do need tons of kit.'

How right he was. This crazy stunt had already cost me two tropical kits and a number six suit.

Within a week we were once again at sea and while en

route to Malta, our first efforts to stalk the enemy began by patrolling the west coast of Italy. After spending a week hugging the shoreline all efforts proved to be fruitless so our captain decided that the north coast of Africa would offer greater rewards for our labours, and so we headed towards Pantelleria. As we turned east we were faced with the problem of penetrating the dreaded minefields between Cape Bon and the southern coast of Sicily. There was no known safe route through the Straits so our submerged boat had to inch its way along, relying entirely on the skill of the asdic operator. The tension in the control room at the time was electrifying. The weird silence was only broken by the sound of the operator's voice as he related his observations to the captain. The captain in turn would order the helmsman to change course accordingly. All was well until we reached the halfway point, then for a few breathtaking seconds we all looked at each other in horror as the sound of heavy wires or metal objects screeched its way along the full length of the hull. Unknown to me then that would not be the only time that I would suffer the same experience. For the next few days further searching for a worthy target proved to be unsuccessful.

It was about 1000 hours when we tied up alongside Lazaretto base in Malta, so being eager to take a breath of fresh air and have a look at our new surroundings a few of us climbed out of the after hatch on to the casing. As I squinted my eyes to get them used to the brilliant sunlight, my attention was drawn to someone shouting my name. As I looked over to the starboard side I could see another 'T' class submarine. She was moored up to a buoy about twenty-five yards away. It was the *Triton*, one of the four submarines that left the UK about the same time as we did. The voice was that of Jack Whiting.

'Shats,' he shouted. 'The *Triad* never made it, she has been lost with all hands, you are very lucky to be alive.'

Whiting and I became friends when we served together aboard the *Dragon* and I had told him of my experiences aboard the *Triad*. The news was one of the worse shocks that I had ever had. Although I had been unhappy during my time aboard her, I couldn't help feeling very remorseful. Less than a month before my former mess-mates had given me moral support when I felt so utterly rejected. Had it not been for a long chain of misdemeanours which had resulted from meeting my old pal Chippy, I would surely have died with them. Although I felt that fate had once again dealt me a lucky hand, it also burdened me with a strong sense of guilt, which in a way enforced a resolute determination for me to face up to danger so as to even the score with my own conscience.

While writing the foreword of Sidney Hart's book, *Discharged Dead*, Commander King posed himself the following question. He wrote, and I quote, 'I can understand what kept officers going, there was the likeli-hood of quick promotion and decorations to spur them on but I could not understand what the lower-deck ratings had to motivate them...' My answer to his question was without a doubt described in the previous paragraph.

Our stay in Malta was short and sweet, just long enough for a few trips ashore while the boat took on fuel water and stores, then once again we were sent on patrol. This time we were heading for the coast of Libya. About a week later our first prey was sighted, she was hugging the coast off Benghazi. It was a sizeable ship, estimated 2,500 tons. But she was not alone. Her formidable escort gave us cause to anticipate that we could be severely punished for our attack. Almost simultaneously with the explosive thuds of two hits scored by our captain, the depth-charges began to rain down on us with frightening accuracy. The enemy's counter-attack was the most severe that I had ever experienced. During the early stage of this attack three of us stood close together in a narrow gangway adjacent to the after-ends. As we stared into each other's faces I made an effort to appear brave by making a wisecrack, but unfortunately and much to my embarrassment my gesture proved just the opposite. As my lips moved up and down like a goldfish, not a sound was forthcoming. Amidst the hilarious laughter I tried desperately to speak. What could have been only a few seconds seemed hours before I could utter a word and laugh with them.

Time after time as the escort came in for the kill we waited and listened for the whirr of her screws closely followed by *tinkle, tinkle, whoom, whoom, whoom*. In the meantime the only evasive action our captain could take was a long process of intermittent 'stop' and 'slow ahead' orders which because of the muffled telegraph gongs, had to be passed by word of mouth from the control room to the motor room. Each time that our pursuers moved so did we. Despite our constant changes of direction the escort doggedly remained in close contact with us and continued to depth-charge us for at least six hours. Then to our relief they withdrew from the attack, I suspect their reason for doing so was because their supply of depth-charges had become exhausted.

Soon after, the buzz ran through the boat that we had been recalled back to Malta. Having survived our recent ordeal, the news was welcomed by all. We entered Lazaretto creek about 0900 a day or so after the recall, and after mooring up to the buoys adjacent to the tip of Manoel Island, half a dozen of us loaded up with mess-traps followed on in single file across the narrow gangway leading to the stone steps of our new base. After passing through a broad archway we stood in the centre of a courtyard. There we were met by the coxswain of the *Perseus* who, pointing to a flight of steps leading up to a veranda, said, 'That is your mess, the one in the corner.'

When I stepped inside the door of our new home I stood on a flagstone floor taking stock of our new surroundings. Sparsely furnished with a long mess table, two bench seats and what looked like luggage racks fixed to the walls, the place looked most austere. We could almost taste the air we breathed as it gave off a dusty unused odour that one associates with empty buildings. From the information that I received at the time I was told that the building had once been used as an isolation hospital and that we were the first people to use it since it closed down. To our delight our new base had one redeeming asset. Being situated on a small island meant we had easy access to the bars and restaurants on Sliema waterfront. I could see before us great hopes and glowing prospects for future relaxation and leisure.

Before we had time to get settled in, a voice from the courtyard bellowed out, 'Come down here the bar is open.'

After paying a visit to the newly improvised oasis which was tucked away in the corner of the courtyard I sat on an empty beer crate supping away on a bottle of blue label. Beer at this time in the morning! I thought to myself, this place will surely be a submariner's Shangri-La. After a thorough scrub out it was time for us off-duty watch to think about celebrating. Contrary to sailors' reports of the seedy activities that one could encounter in the street of steps, alias 'The Gut', I personally experienced nothing more harmful than inebriated sailors occasionally parting with their sixpenny pieces to buy a glass of coloured water in order to sit next to a female who was prepared to listen to all their moans and groans of the day. As for other highly coloured exploits, I would regard them as being figments of imagination in the minds of sprog sailors who need something to blow about. Some may have other opinions, but these were the findings of someone so green that I should have worn a cabbage for a button hole.

Shame on any self-respecting sailor who served in the Med at that time had not met the two characters, Bobby and Sugar. Both of these people would describe themselves as cabaret artists. Although I had met and spoken to them many times, I never once saw them perform anything like a song and dance routine. But with regards their talents as comics, that is another story. Sugar was massive, he would turn the scales at sixteen stone. This heavy-featured hulk of muscle was adorned with lipstick and eye shadow and dressed in skin tight black silk trousers which were complemented by his feminine-looking blouse. Far from being a sexual turn on, it had to be a laugh. Whatever their profession, they became objects of friendly ridicule but it never seemed to worry them.

A typical run ashore would begin with a jaunty hike to the far end of the island, then crossing a small footbridge we would make for the ever open doors of the Blue Heaven bar which was situated directly opposite. Being near at hand it was always a good starting point for a binge. From there on we would move from bar to bar until we sampled at least six of them on Sliema seafront. Usually by the evening we were pretty well steamed up and in fine fettle to make a final assault down the Gut. Although there was no shortage of bars in other zones on the island, the Gut offered a greater concentration of them. In this street of terraced steps every other building was a so-called cabaret bar.

It was usual practice to kick off in the Gyppo Queen, the word Gyppo of course being Jolly Jack's distortion of Egyptian. Regarding the names of other bars, very few escaped a transformation in one form or another but the one that I thought was most amusing was the Galvanised donkey, Jacks version of the Silver Horse.

After a short stay in the New Life and Lucky Wheel, it would be time for big eats in Charlie's restaurant, and often one felt a bit green about the gills by this time, but this made no difference to Charlie. He would be standing in the doorway ready to waylay every prospective customer. Presenting himself with the most disarming smile and while crying out, 'Inside Stokes, big eats inside,' he would almost drag you over the threshold. Whether you wanted food or not, you would feel obliged to respond to his warm and friendly greeting, then having done so there were no regrets. For a couple of shillings a sailor could feast on steak, egg and chips rounded off with a glass of wine, a small cigar and a box of matches. Charlie was not only the tout, he was also the cook and waiter. With such enthusiasm for business he would put modern restaurateurs to shame, especially when it came to speedy service. The fast food was managed from a tiny stove tucked away in the smallest of kitchens, all this he achieved with no help whatsoever. Before leaving, Charlie would have to be assured that you were satisfied with the meal and that you would come again. He would then lead you to the door, wave goodnight and leave you to continue to guzzle beer in the either of the two remaining bars, namely the United Services, or the Bull and Bush.

For the timid, it was time to seek refuge for the night. This service was provided by Charlie senior who owned the lodging house next door to the restaurant and there for a shilling you could sleep the night away in a nice clean bed. Having suffered such a binge, three of us were awakened by Charlie's father and as usual he provided each of us with a glass of lime juice.

'Haven't you got anything stronger?' I asked.

'Sure,' he said. 'Give me the money and I will get you anything you want.' A few minutes later he would return with a large bottle of scotch. We then poured its contents into the now empty glasses then each of us with one swallow guzzled the lot. We then decided to get another bottle for the road and after taking another few swills I stuffed the remaining half a bottle down my jumper. Then the three of us staggered into Charlie's for breakfast.

During the meal Charlie's fruit and veg supplier walked through to the kitchen, supporting a large crate of cauliflowers on his head. Remembering the shortage of vegetables during our last patrol, I asked him to get a crate for us to take back to the boat. I then suggested that we should find a gharri driver who was prepared to take us and the cauliflowers back to our base on Maneol Island. Very soon he returned with the veg and informed us that the gharri was waiting in the side street round the corner.

After lashing the crate to the top of the gharri we set off on our journey. Joe Grisdale and Tom Waterworth were seated inside the cab, while I after much protesting from the cab driver managed to secure a position in the front seat beside him. By now the whisky had taken over and we were all three sheets to the wind, so relishing a little fun I struggled with the driver to take over the reins. As we were about to round the corner by the opera house the poor bewildered nag broke into a gallop and went charging towards a huge crowd of people who was gathered in the square before going to Sunday morning Mass. Instead of completing the turn round the corner the whole caboodle shot across the road on two wheels, it then mounted the pavement and came to rest with a sudden jolt when we collided with a tree which stood in the centre of a huge patio. The ranting driver was ejected from his seat and came to rest half sprawled across the back of the poor old nag which was at that time down on his front knees saying his morning prayers. Then having slid to the ground the driver took to his heels and went charging into the crowd like a mad dog.

In the meantime my two mates were having a whale of a time as they stood among the cauliflowers tossing their hats in the air and calling 'Yippee' to all and sundry. By now we had become the centre of attraction for hordes of Sunday morning worshippers. To them our antics must have looked like a wild west rodeo show. Through hazy eyes I gazed over the heads of the multitudes and in the distance I managed to pick out the forms of the shore patrol men. As they made haste towards us it became quite clear to me that they were not there as spectators, they had been sent there to try and break up our little party. As they came near to us I climbed into the tree and began to take large swigs from the bottle of whisky which I still had tucked away inside my jumper. As I did so, the leading hand of the patrol had reached a spot directly beneath me and tried to grab at my feet, and at the same time he was screaming his lungs out for me to come down.

'If you want me, come up and get me,' I shouted between gulps.

Although my mates were already in custody I still sat high in the heart of the tree and not before my bottle was empty did I decide to come down. As soon as my feet touched the ground I was whisked away and thrown into the waiting wagon along with the other two. When the doors slammed shut behind us I took my last look at our audience. There must have been a thousand people late for Mass that day. Within a few minutes we were inside the Picket House being questioned by the master-at-arms who was sitting behind his desk in the centre of the room.

'I want your names, official numbers and your ship,' he demanded. Although he seemed satisfied with the answers offered by Grisdale and myself, he began to show signs of distress when questioning Waterworth.

Out of the blue Tom had suddenly adopted an Eton accent. 'I am Sir Thomas Charles Waterworth, and I want to phone my solicitors immediately,' he stated. His claim to the title sounded so convincing that I almost believed it myself.

Soon the Jaunty decided that he had heard enough and had us all put behind bars for safe keeping while he phoned our commanding officer. We hadn't been there long before nature called upon us to empty our bladders and having been refused the use of the toilets the pain became so severe that we could no longer suffer the agony, so in desperation I began to urinate on a pile of straw pallets that were stacked in the corner. My solution to the problem quickly caught on, when one by one my cell-mates relieved themselves in the same way. By this time the full effects of the whisky had taken toll of our senses as we spread the saturated mattresses out on the cell floor and took refuge in the land of nod. Sometime later we were wakened by the sound of voices outside the cell. As we staggered to our feet we were cheerfully greeted by our new escort which consisted of half a dozen men chosen from our mess-mates on the boat. Through blurred vision I recognised one of them as Stoker Gilliam-Hill.

Grinning all over his chops he asked, 'What have you buggers been up to?' It was obvious that our mess-mates thought our situation was hilarious. They just couldn't stop laughing. After telling us that they had been detailed to take us back to the boat they asked if we were going to come quietly, after we had convinced them that we had our fun and would be no more trouble they unlocked the cell door and took us out to the waiting wagon. During the next few days remorse became the predominant emotion. After being formally charged by the first lieutenant the three of us were given plenty of time to sweat it out before being weighed off by the captain. In due time he made it quite clear that he was not amused. The fact that there was no spare crew to relieve us must have contributed towards his decision not to send us to choky. Instead we were made to pay for new mattresses and confined to the boat for fourteen days, since we would be going out on patrol long before that, it didn't seem to matter much.

Ever since our arrival at the new base I had been troubled with what I first thought to be mosquito bites. These bites had become progressively more irritating as each day passed. They first appeared after I had slept on a kapok bedspread which someone had left on the wall-racks. During a heavy sleep after a binge ashore I could vaguely remember being bitten several times, but it was not until daylight that I realised to what extent. After a few days the bites had developed into scabby ulcers and I was obliged to seek medical advice. The MO's diagnosis was that the infection was caused by the predatory work of the sandfly. Early next morning I was taken by ambulance to Intaffa Hospital, which to me seemed to be a bit of a makeshift establishment annex to a military base in the centre of the island.

Soon after my arrival I was subjected to examination by another MO. After confirming the first diagnosis he turned towards the male nurse and gave him instructions for my treatment. First he said I must have a hot sulphur bath. I was then taken to a bathroom and told to step into a bath of near boiling water. After a soaking I was handed a large jar of sulphur and a purser's hard scrubbing brush. I was then told to scrub the sulphur into the open sores. After this agonising treatment I was given a flannel suit to wear.

'You must keep it on for twenty-four hours,' the nurse told me.

I was then taken to a small ward occupied by no more than three others, a French sailor, an army sergeant, and one Maltese civilian. It was not long before we were socialising round a pot of tea.

'What is wrong with you?' asked the sergeant.

'Well I don't know really. I picked up a bug somewhere and now my body is covered with sores,' I answered.

At that moment my attention was drawn towards the

teacups, I had noticed that each handle had a different colour tag tied to it. The sergeant's reaction was most reassuring.

'Oh don't worry about us,' he said. 'You are in excellent company we have all caught syph.' He then burst out laughing as I almost choked on a mouthful of tea which I was about to swallow.

The next day I was told to take another hot bath, but this time I was given a jar of brown ointment and told to rub it all over my body. The stuff was most revolting, it looked and smelt like human excretion, the smell was so vile that I was even ostracised by the other three patients who, as the sergeant had boasted, were only here because they were unlucky sportsmen. That, I thought, was a downright insult to me. Although I had thought the treatment to be rather primitive it proved to be very effective because after a few days the itching had stopped and the sores were well on the way to healing. Very soon I was on my way back to Manoel Island with all the expectations of rejoining the *Tetrarch*, but to my dismay she was out on patrol. This meant that my chances of rejoining her now was very slim indeed. I instinctively knew that I would be drafted to one of the older boats of which far too many had been lost.

Chapter Six

The Peanut

Within a week my hunch had developed into reality. The *Tetrarch* was still at sea and I was given a draft chit to the s/m *Parthian* or more affectionately known to her crew as the *Peanut*. Although the boat itself had seen better days it had two redeeming assets. First its captain, Commander Rimmington, a seasoned submariner, had already proved himself to be a formidable opponent to the enemy. His latest was an Italian submarine which he torpedoed and sunk off the coast of Tobruk. Secondly the boat contained that sought-after and rare commodity during that period, namely a mature crew, who had enjoyed a wealth of experience in both peace- and wartime operations.

During my first conversations with my mess-mates I made no secret of my displeasure in joining them, and my constant appraisals of the *Tetrarch* and its crew started to raise a few eyebrows. Needless to say that I was duly rewarded with a barrage of good-humoured jibes and comments.

When it came to leg-pulling, Leading Stoker Pip Piper was a real expert. Flaunting his cockney humour he would often wink at me and taunt me with the words, 'It is not as good as was on the *Tetrarch*.' The subject in question could have been anything from the food on the table or as far-reaching as the time taken for the gunlayer to let go five rounds. He never missed an opportunity to have a go at me.

The mirth created by his humorous taunts made him the loveable character that he was.

I recall memories of the first day that I joined the *Parthian*. Almost as soon as I presented myself to Chief Stoker Lee, he told me to change into my number 1s and join the rest of the boat's crew on a makeshift parade ground at the rear of the base. There the ship's company was formed into two ranks. After reporting to the captain that the ship's company was present and correct, the first lieutenant took up his position at the head of the other officers who were standing in a single rank to the left of the crew. Up to this moment I hadn't a clue what was happening. The events which followed marred my day with sombre thoughts which would keep me on the straight and narrow for sometime to come.

The sound of marching feet brought my attention to a prisoner who was attired in unlaced boots, a plain white canvas sailor's suit and cap. He was escorted by a guard on each side with the coxswain following. Upon reaching a position a few paces in front of the captain, the coxswain shouted the order, 'Prisoner and escort, halt.' Then for a few agonising seconds the silence became eerie whilst we stood rigidly to attention staring at the unfortunate captive before us. The stillness was interrupted by the sound of the coxswain's command 'Off cap.' As the prisoner stood bare-headed, the charge was read aloud. His motionless figure gave way to a nervous twitch in his cheeks as the captain sentenced him to ninety days in a military prison. The prisoner was then escorted back to his cell and we on parade were dismissed.

Turning to one of my mess-mates I asked, 'Who was that?'

He answered, 'That was the man that you have just replaced, so be warned, don't go lashing out at officers.'

Towards the end of December I began my first patrol on

the *Parthian*. The duties that I had been assigned to were in the engine room for both patrol routine, (i.e. surface running) and watch diving. From my first observations I could not help comparing the neat compact layout of a 'T' class engine room, with the huge and clumsy clapped out diesels which seemed to be closing in on me, and I found the noise that they generated terrifying. At the expense of a full quota of bunks, the stokers' mess was more spacious than that of the *Tetrarch*, so being the last stoker to join the boat I was denied the privilege of sleeping in a bunk. Instead I was given the option of sleeping on a foot wide mess-stool or on the deck beneath the table. I chose the latter.

One morning when I came off watch I stepped into the mess with all expectations of enjoying a hearty breakfast of eggs and bacon which I had seen carried through the engine room into the mess half an hour before.

'Where's mine?' I asked one of the lads.

'It's on the shelf at the back of the mess,' came the reply.

'My favourite bacon and eggs,' I answered. As I sat down at the table I looked at my plate I could see that the frying fat had congealed round the edge of the plate.

'What idiot put my breakfast under the fan?' I asked. But I could have saved my breath because no one answered. I was half way through the meal when I noticed a few footprints in the fat round the edge of the plate.

When I pointed it out to Stoker Shepherd, he smiled and said, 'I shouldn't eat any more if I were you, it looks as though the rats have been at it.' For a moment I thought he was kidding but I was soon to learn otherwise.

It was during a long dive a few days later when I was startled by the figure of Jimmy Binns flying through mid-air. He had taken a gigantic leap from his bunk and after screaming like a hyena he stood shaking like a jelly in the middle of the mess-deck.

'Those bloody rats, one of them ran right across my chest,' he cried out. Poking my head up from underneath the table I almost wet my pants laughing at him. He in turn got so bloody mad I thought I had better pack up before he thumped me.

'I am not sleeping there no more,' he said.

'I don't see what there is to worry about,' I replied.

'If you are so bloody brave perhaps you would like to change places with me,' he challenged.

I immediately seized the opportunity to crash down in a nice comfortable bunk and for a long while I was quite happy with the new arrangement. Between watches I would often lie in my bunk and listen to the squeaks of young rats and it was my guess that they were nesting behind the panel just above my head. Now and again the squeaks would be interrupted by a flurry of tiny feet as the adults chased each other over the top of the plywood panels. Despite the rodents' capers I had no problem with sleeping. As they squeaked away I would close my eyes and imagine that I was surrounded by caged canaries.

As the days passed, the condition of the main engines was progressively worsening and by mid-patrol we had replaced two cracked cylinder heads and one cylinder liner on the starboard engine. This was followed by two big-end bearings on the port engine. In doing so we used up all our spares, so we were unable to replace another big-end which partially crippled the port engine. This latest breakdown was over come by disconnecting the big-end bearing from the main shaft and suspending the piston from the deck-head. By isolating the whole unit we were able to run the engine on seven cylinders instead of eight. A huge split in the exhaust manifold cooling water jacket on the starboard engine did little to improve our comfort. This fractured water jacket caused the temperature in the engine room to soar above one hundred and twenty degrees.

Because of their massive size, repairs to these engines required the use of large chain blocks for hoisting the huge components and pulley block ropes which was ingeniously rigged to enable us to haul the massive spanners required to fasten down the huge nuts on the cylinder heads. It can be appreciated that this work was performed in a confined space with no overhead room to manoeuvre. Working in these extreme temperatures, all modesty was thrown to the winds, our only attire would be a pair of sandals or perhaps a pair of football shorts or a loin cloth worn around our middles.

Despite major problems in the engine room, Commander Rimmington's determination to complete our mission did not waver. Although we lost time because our captain thought it was expedient to withdraw to deeper waters in order to carry out repairs, as soon as those repairs were completed he closed into the narrow Straits of Messina and continued to keep periscope watches, thus remaining ever vigilant for any sign of enemy shipping. As for our part, in the engine room life had become one long continual slog as we sought desperately to cope with the ever-increasing repairs. The tasks demanded the utmost care because it was vital to maintain strict silence during the operations. There was no easy solution to this problem, every tool and each piece of heavy equipment had to be placed on the steel deckplates with the minimum amount of noise. Being close to enemy shores any metallic clanging would be picked up by the anti-submarine patrol vessels and that would spell disaster. During this time the strong current pouring through the Messina Straits had caused all sorts of problems for both the periscope and hydroplane watchkeepers. The continual strain of holding the boat's position against the flow of the fast running tides and at the same time maintaining efficient periscope depth had gradually depleted the charge in the batteries.

It was during the second week of the patrol that an early morning mist became a welcome bonus for Commander Rimmington. It enabled him to remain on the surface for longer than it was otherwise safe to do so. As the morning gave way to brilliant sunlight, our captain gave the order, 'Dive, Dive, Dive.' To the sound of the klaxon, the conning tower hatch was slammed shut and the main vents swung open. As the boat dived the needle on the diving gauge swung to twenty feet, there was a sudden jar which threw us all off balance as the sound of the boat's keel tore deep into the steel structure of an uncharted submerged wreck. Realising that visibility was increasing rapidly and that our bridge was exposed to shore gun batteries required some quick thinking, which our captain was able to provide. With both main motors 'grouped up' (full power) he ordered 'full astern both,', 'stop both,', 'full astern,' and so on. Although these manoeuvres caused the boat to shake from bow to stern we still remained entangled in the wreck. All attempts to free ourselves by blowing main ballast tanks failed. For an agonising three quarters of an hour we remained trapped as we tried to squirm free from the obstruction. As both main motors continued to roar away we all realised that our depleted batteries could not take this kind of punishment for very much longer. As we were faced with the possibilities of being blown to pieces at any second, the old *Peanut* sent her roaring screws on their final bid to break free. Then suddenly with the sound of screeching metal we bounced off the wreck as free as an escaped balloon. With our batteries almost on the point of collapse our captain withdrew from the Straits of Messina and set course toward Cape Spartivento.

During that period one of our favourite topics was our adopted pets, the rats. Someone had noticed that every time that we were dismissed from diving stations one of the rats would run along the HP air lines towards the stokers' mess-deck. It had been seen so often that we swore it went to diving stations. One morning after we had been given the order 'Fall out diving stations,' there was no sign of it, so a few of us stayed behind waiting for it to show. After a few seconds Pip Piper bounced into the engine room and in his usual jubilant manner he turned to us and said, 'What are you waiting for? Do you not want to get your heads down?' After explaining that we were waiting for the rat to show up, Pip's eyes lit up with devilment as he retorted, 'I am going to kill that bastard.'

'You will do nothing of the kind,' snapped Jan Leach. 'Don't you know it is lucky to have rats aboard a ship,' he added.

But Jan's West Country superstition meant nothing to Pip who immediately picked up the gauntlet. In defiance of Jan's plea, early next morning Pip meticulously lined up a long-handled broom between some pipes so that the end of the handle was two inches away from the rat's run, then after waiting for the poor creature to make its run, he gave the hairy end of the broom one almighty blow thus splattering the rat's skull all over the bulkhead. When the news of this atrocity reached Jan Leach, his face went deathly white. His reaction only added to Pip's amusement as he stood there soaking up Jan's verbal attack while the rest of us crippled ourselves with laughter. The whole scene became so comical, it was rather like Saturday night at the Hippodrome, billing Jan and Pip as the star performers.

No sooner had the mess quietened down when the tannoy blurted out the order 'diving stations'. Up top it was daylight so the order could only mean one thing. We must have sighted the enemy. As Jan leapt from his bunk he cried out, 'I told you what would happen, now we are for it.'

But this time there was no response to his outcry, we were far too busy rushing to our diving stations. During an attack the engine room became a convenient place for a few of us to gather. The reason being that the foremost water-tight door was in close proximity to the control room so it was handy for one of us to creep through and observe the attack. We could then pass all relative information along the grapevine. On this occasion we had learned that the captain had been shadowing a ten thousand ton tanker and two smaller supply ships. The convoy was escorted by one of the Italian's most modern sloops which imposed a severe threat to any would-be attacker that hadn't done his homework. Undaunted by the prospect of certain retaliation our captain scored at least two hits. There was probably a third but the first pattern of depth-charges which almost lifted the engine room hatch from its hinges, made it impossible for us to distinguish the explosions.

This frenzied counter-attack continued for many hours resulting with several leaks throughout the boat. Although most of the depth gauges had been shut off for deep diving, still a few were broken. The spider clips on the engine room hatch were causing those of us below it to suffer a few anxious moments as each explosion caused the hatch to lift, showering us with water. Back aft, the situation was worse. Stoker Shepherd had a full-time job trying to cope with the amount of water which was flowing freely through the stern glands, after the hydroplanes had taken the full blast of one pattern of depth-charges. The explosion caused them to buckle and become jammed thereby putting the boat at a tail-down angle at a depth of four hundred feet. As we waited in dead silence between each pattern of depth-charges, we stared at each other's faces as the excess pressure on the hull caused it to creak and groan under the intense battering it was receiving. The damage to the after planes made it impossible for the hydroplane watchkeepers to control the trim from the control room, but after changing over to a secondary method the after-end watchkeeper managed to free the planes long enough to put the boat on level trim. But still the depth-charges came raining down on us.

In the meantime the captain ordered all machinery to be stopped and started at intervals which were timed to coincide with the movements of the enemy above. The use of the clanging telegraphs was abandoned and all orders from the control room to the motor room were passed by word of mouth. Having nothing to do myself I squatted on one of the ERA's tool boxes trying my damnedest to continue reading my current book. It was the story of Ben Hur and the fact that I had my head buried in it for two hours and did not turn a single page had not gone unnoticed by my fellow sufferers. This incident gave rise to a few wisecracks which created a little mirth and a slight relief at a time when it was most needed. It was now four or five hours since we first made contact with the enemy but gradually our captain's tactics were beginning to pay dividends as he cunningly outwitted the persistent pursuit of the anti-submarine patrol vessel, and by late afternoon we were out of immediate danger.

The order 'Fall out diving stations' came as a great relief and looking round at my mess-mates I could see that the stress of the day's events had clearly taken a toll on their faces. In just a few hours young men seemed to have aged far beyond their years. Perhaps the one exception was Pip Piper who stepped into the engine room just as perky as ever. Then slapping me on the shoulder he scoffed, 'What do you think of the old *Peanut* now?'

'Not too bad,' I replied. Then seeking to restore my pride I lied when I taunted him, 'It wasn't as big as the ship we sunk off Benghazi in the *Tetrarch*.' At that moment Jan Leach stepped through the watertight door to join in the pantomime. In a fit of rage he pointed to Pip and cried out, 'It was your bloody fault, I suppose you are satisfied now, I told you not to kill that bloody rat.'

Pip's good-humoured but provocative reply only added fuel to the fire which flared up with a further outburst of fury from Jan who was now unwittingly acting as straight man in one of Pip's star performances. When Jan finally realised that we were all having a good laugh at his expense, he stormed through the engine room shouting out behind him, 'You are all raving mad, the bloody lot of you.'

On a more serious note I turned to Pip and asked him why they called the boat the *Peanut*.

'Haven't you seen those bloody great letters on the side of the conning tower?' he mocked. This was of course for quick recognition, PN being short for *Parthian*.

We had now retreated to the safety of deeper waters but our troubles were by no means over. The severe damage caused by the explosions resulted in the continuous jamming of the after planes giving the watchkeepers a hard time as they struggled to keep the boat in trim back aft, the port main propeller shaft thrust bearing block had become almost detached from the hull, which was badly distorted due to the sea pressure when we were forced to dive deep. Because of this the whole of the port shaft had been thrown out of alignment with the thrust bearing taking most of the punishment. It had become so hot that the watchkeepers were unable to touch it. Despite this we managed to keep the white metal bearings from seizing by constantly replenishing the boiling lubrication oil with new cool oil and so keep the port shaft operational. All this, together with damaged steering, was not the ideal condition in which to start an eight hundred mile trip back to our base in Alexandria. Perhaps this was the reason the captain broke our journey by calling in at the Greek port Piraeus.

For whatever reason, news of this unexpected visit came as a pleasant surprise. After three weeks at sea a run ashore was always welcome but the excitement of visiting a port where I had never been before added to my interest. As always on ships you can rely on someone who knows his way around in a strange port. This time it was Stoker Shepherd. In just a few minutes he was able to advise us with good authority what it was like in Athens which is just a few miles away from Piraeus. His description was most encouraging. A few hours later he proved his knowledge by steering us towards all those elegant bars and disreputable dives often frequented by seafaring moderates. But unfortunately our frolics were short-lived.

As I recall, the mood of the city during the first day of our stay seemed quite stable. The hustle and bustle of traffic and the trading in the shops seemed no different than one would expect in a city outside the war zone. Such was my impression at that time, but all this was to change drastically within twenty-four hours. During the morning of the second day I stood on the casing taking a breath of fresh air and soon became aware of a remarkable change in our surroundings. Many ships had moved out overnight and other smaller craft were getting ready to leave. As I looked on I became depressed with the chilling feeling that a huge cloud of expectancy had descended over the whole harbour. Although the surrender of Athens to our common enemy was still a few days away the writing was on the wall. However our captain knew a lot more than I did. This became obvious when he stopped all shore leave and ordered the boat to be secured for sea.

With much of our machinery still crippled, we were now faced with the daunting prospect of battling our way through hostile seas for the remaining four hundred miles back to Alexandria. Once at sea, we came face to face with the innumerable problems in the engine room. Although much of the damage had been repaired, we were now being plagued with a spate of new breakdowns which continued to develop after each night run on the surface. Each morning, as soon as we had submerged, a team of ERAs would descend on the offending parts of the machinery with all the vigour of burrowing beavers. As for my part in these operations I received the fastest and most exacting course in engineering that one could conceivably imagine. In just one month my skills had widened. From a non-participant, I had blossomed into a first class diesel mechanic, capable of fitting any component on the engines. By the time the boat had reached Alexandria I had become a trusted member of a skilful team who together had exchanged one cylinder liner, two breach-ends and three big-ends. For good measure we had nursed the port engine with its isolated unit for four hundred miles and completed no end of decarbonising jobs on the exhaust valves.

As soon as the boat was tied up alongside the *Medway*, half a dozen of us stokers climbed up on to the casing. As I tried to view my new surroundings the morning sun was blinding me. With squinting eyes I searched the faces of my fellow shipmates. Did the brilliant sunlight exaggerate their haggard looks? I didn't think so. Their appearance was ample testimony to the gruesome experience we had suffered during the past few weeks. Dressed in shorts and sandals we presented ourselves as perfect examples of dejected humanity. Having taken up position alongside that fine parent ship mother *Medway*, the *Parthian* was completely dwarfed by her huge bulk. It was a most spacious ship that was capable of parenting at least ten submarines at any one time. It was commanded by Captain Ruck-Keene who at that time faced the unenviable task of spreading his charges far too thinly, therefore it was not surprising to find only two more submarines alongside us.

As I collected some of the mess-traps to take inboard, Pip Piper with his usual good humour taunted me with the news that the *Tetrarch* was one of the other submarines that was sheltered alongside the *Medway*. The news delighted me as I could not wait to see my old shipmates. The first one that I met was Stoker Gilliam-Hill who already knew as much as I did about the *Parthian*'s latest assault on the enemy. This was made obvious when he patted me on the shoulder and congratulated me. Although I had played only a meagre role in the operation his gesture made me feel quite proud.

By mutual arrangement my partner for my first run ashore in Alexandria was a wild-looking character who came from Galway. From his appearance I could well imagine him to be of hardy stock who had earned his living by braving the stormy seas off the West Coast of Ireland. His name was Michael Le-Haine, or more affectionately, 'Mad Mick'. His long aquiline nose was almost hidden by a deluge of smoke from a bucket-sized bowl on the end of his pipe stem. He owned the most weird collection of pipes that I have ever seen. These he kept filled with the most repugnant smelling tobacco which kept me on constant alert to keep to his lee side. As I was sitting dressed, awaiting the liberty boat, Jimmy Binns asked me who I was going ashore with. When I told him, his lips parted in a broad grin as he commented, 'That could be trouble for you.' Unshaken, I did not take heed of his warning and as soon as we set foot ashore we began to top up on Stella beer with all the avidity of two parched desert camels. Fortunately there was no shortage of beer in the Fleet Club but glasses to drink out of were non-existent. We were told that a shipload of Aussies had visited the club a week before and had left their calling cards. A shipment of new glasses to replace those that were broken were understandably well down the Admiralty's priority list. So for the next two years we suffered the discomfort of having to drink out of dark brown bottles with their tops sawn off.

Towards the evening Mick began to get a bit fidgety and suggested that we should move on towards the cabaret in

Beer Street. When we arrived there, we sat down at a table near the dance floor and it was not long before we were being entertained by a cluster of scantily clad dancing girls and as I gazed at their flabby bellies I could only regard them with some distaste. Little did I realise that within two hours and a bottle of brandy those self same girls would become raving beauties. However by that time I was in no fit state to treat myself to such luxuries and less able to afford it. The next morning I was awakened by the sound of ringing bells and as I opened my eyes I saw a man dressed in a long white robe with a fez perched on top off his head. He seemed to get a lot of pleasure seeing me cringe in agony as he stood in the doorway shaking the bell for all its worth. In the room I counted six beds occupied by an equal number of sailors, none of whom I knew. As each of them became mobile I noticed that they all had swollen eyes.

I spoke to one of them asking, 'What happened to you lot, have you all been in a punch-up?'

'No,' he answered. 'It's those bloody mosquitoes, how come that they have not bitten you?'

'I guess they didn't like the smell of the brandy,' I answered.

A few minutes later when I was sitting in the tea bar when my eyes beheld the most unlovely sight. It was 'Mick'. Still in a drunken stupor, he staggered over to my table and flopped into a chair. The brandy must have burned his throat out because he was so hoarse that he could hardly speak. It was soon time to be getting back to the boat. As we passed through the tall iron gates that led to the street, Mick stopped to buy a bunch of flowers and a local newspaper.

Somewhat puzzled, I asked, 'Why on earth did you buy those?' For a sailor to buy flowers seemed rare enough but what was his reason for buying an Egyptian paper? I hadn't a clue why he should want a paper that he could not read. I had not long to wait for an explanation, that's if you can call it one. I could not believe my eyes when he picked off the blooms and devoured them. That seemed odd enough but when he tore off a piece of the front page of the newspaper and ate it, I immediately realised why they called him 'Mad Mick'. As soon as we arrived back on board, we welcomed the news that the boat was going to Port Said for a refit but even more pleasing was the news that the whole crew had been invited to spend a week on the luxurious houseboat *Puritan* which was moored on the Nile in Cairo.

Within a few days our boat stood wedged between the blocks in Port Fuad. I was one of eight stokers who had been chosen to take first leave. Having journeyed east by rail the wheels of the train ground to a halt about lunchtime. As it did so a crowd of Arabs surged toward the dusty tracks and as they came near us we could hear their rhythmic chanting, 'Eggs and bread, eggs and bread.'

'How much?' I shouted.

Almost immediately a group of them pushed their way to the front and became engaged in fierce competition with each other as they tried to flog us their wares. The train remained stationary just long enough for us to amuse ourselves by teasing and bartering with the unsuspecting vendors and it was not until they drastically reduced their price to rock bottom that we told them to stuff their eggs and bread because we didn't want their fly-infected food at any price. At least that is what we meant, even though we did word it differently. As the train pulled away we saluted the protesting Arabs with two fingers. Not very good ambassadors I know but that is how it was.

From Cairo station we took a short journey by coach to the outskirts of the city and then for a mile or so along the banks of the Nile where the coach stopped in front of an immaculate white-painted houseboat which was to be our residence for the next five days. We boarded the vessel by means of a short gangway which spanned above a small but well-attended garden which sloped from the mooring bank down to the water's edge. Indeed the whole setting looked very promising for an enjoyable time for the next few days. Life on this floating hotel was most luxurious and having never experienced anything like it before I was most impressed by the way that the other half lived. Our hosts were the members of the Gezira Sporting Club. Lord and Lady Lampton and Thomas Cook's chief administrator in Cairo were among a few members who came aboard to welcome us. During the conversation Lady Lampton confessed that when she heard that a submarine crew was coming there, she couldn't wait to see what we were like. I think that she expected to see us wearing black eye-patches and brandishing cutlasses. She seemed so disappointed when we behaved almost like gentlemen.

All too soon we were back on the boat in Port Fuad and up to our necks in oil and grime. Once again we had to face up to the reality of war and very soon our week of luxurious living had become a fading memory. When we returned we found that the civilian dockyard engineers had been given the responsibility of making good our damaged machinery and all the welding to our split tanks. New rubber seals were fitted to the engine room hatch and as an extra precaution against future depth-charging, each hatch was equipped with four heavy dog-clips the like of which had been fitted to the *Tetrarch* and other 'T' class boats from new. Other menial work provided the crew with employment during the days, leaving us ample time to let off steam in the evenings. It was now three years since I had paid a short visit to Port Said so when it was time to renew my acquaintance with the varied entertainments that the port had to offer, I was feeling quite excited.

At 1600 hours Geordie Heddon, Ted Hooks, Scouse

Shepherd and myself boarded the ferry boat which would take us on a half mile trip from Port Fuad to Port Said. It was a nice warm evening so we decided to take refuge under a huge brolly that sprouted from the centre of the table which was situated on the front patio on the main street. We hadn't been seated long before we were being entertained by the sleight of hand which was expertly displayed by the gillie-gillie man. Under our watchful eyes this magician conjured from thin air half a dozen chicks which ended up happily hopping all over the table. After half an hour or so, three of us looked at Shepherd who had just announced, 'Drink up lads and I will take you to see the monks.'

'What monks?' I gasped.

'Don't look so worried,' he said, 'there's a nice club just round the corner. You'll like it.'

I couldn't help feeling a little apprehensive about his choice of night spots. Could this holy sanctuary provide seasoned sailors with the type of entertainment to which they were accustomed, I wondered? However we all decided to give it a whirl and within a few minutes we were jaunting our way in a gharri towards the club. As we stood in the entrance surveying the prospects we were approached by two Franciscan monks. The elder of the two was a tall lean man and his apparent advancing years could well excuse the slight stoop in his bearing. His long curved nose barely supported his silver framed thick lens glasses which hung at the most precarious angle. With folded arms he shuffled in his sandals towards us, then peering over the top of his glasses, he greeted us with a friendly smile.

As he beckoned us inside he said, 'Come in boys and make yourselves comfortable, we have a nice bar down at the other end.'

In contrast to the old monk's friendly welcome his younger brother seemed to regard us with an air of suspicion. Perhaps this was not too surprising because sailors were not always plaster saints while ashore in foreign lands. When we arrived at the bar we were greeted by an equally friendly woman who we later came to know as Mrs Maxwell. After chatting with her we learned that she was born in Malta but had lived in Port Said for many years. She also told us that she was married to a Scotsman who was the chief accountant for the Suez Canal Company. During the next few weeks we became frequent visitors to the RC club and the monks seemed quite happy to provide us with excellent white wine at the knock-down price of two shillings a bottle. After a while our nightly tipple had progressed from one bottle to four bottles each, so we were well on the way to becoming 'winos'. Each night we would stagger back to the boat as high as kites and very soon we were appropriately labelled the four vin-blonkers which of course was Jolly Jack's distortion of vin blanc.

As we came to know the old monk better, we realised that he was not quite the simpleton as one may have suspected, he could in fact speak eight languages fluently and at one time he had been attached to the French Foreign Legion. When I asked him if legionnaires were as tough as their reputation sometimes portrayed, such as in the story *Beau Geste*, he answered by saying, 'Perhaps they would sometimes become a little unruly when returning to town after being stationed at an outpost, but on the whole they would only be out to enjoy themselves, much the same as you lads.'

But for his training in diplomacy, he may well have said that, 'They were no bloody worse than you lot.' Although he would always come over for a chat we could never persuade him to take a drink with us. He in turn would ask us to go to Sunday Mass in the cathedral where he was the resident priest. But alas each Sunday evening he would shake his head and say, 'I never saw you at Mass this morning.'

One night Hooks, Heddon, and myself were making tracks towards the RC Club when Blimp Jennings and Batchy Bartlet two of the *Parthian*'s ERAs offered us a ride on a flat-topped truck which they had purloined from a side street.

'Hop on stokes, we will give you a ride,' they shouted. So relishing anything for a bit of fun the three of us obliged. It wasn't long before the heavy truck began to gather momentum. As it raced down a steep incline with all the force of a Roman chariot, the two silly sods let go of the shaft, and the next thing I knew the truck was upside down leaving us three stokers half unconscious moaning and groaning in the gutter. The next day I could vaguely remember the two tiffys leaning over us saying, 'Leave them there, they will be all right when they come to.'

On the following Saturday the old monk once again declined our invitation to join us for a drink, but this time he played his trump card. 'I have an idea,' he said. 'If you all come to Mass tomorrow morning we can then all have lunch in the rectory, and there I will join you in a drink.' This was an offer that we could not refuse. The old boy had made a bargain with the devil. At 1000 hours the following morning, we four saintly converts stepped off the ferry and strolled along the promenade towards Port Said's beautiful cathedral. Then as we drew near to the vestibule my eyes beheld the jubilant figure of the old monk. His beaming smile made it clear to us that he had won the day, at least that is what he thought. I chuckled to myself while thinking that he had yet to fulfil his half of the bargain. Soon after the service was over our saintly host rejoined us and after conducting us on a tour round the cathedral, he took us to his dining room. Having wined and dined and wined well into the evening, we four self-satisfied conspirers sat gloating over our achievement, as the old monk sat at the end of the table giggling like a naughty schoolboy. Eventually when the old monk showed signs that he could take no more, I, along with my conniving colleagues, decided to call it a day. By then our host had completely run out of steam, so the only decent thing for us to do was to take him to his cell and turn him in for the night. After removing his brown habit we helped him up on to his bunk and left him in peace. One most moving memory that I still retain in my mind was my last look at him, as he laid there in a spotless clean white cell. He was garbed in an immaculate white undergarment with nothing other than the cross of Christ hung on a bare wall to keep him company. He was the nearest thing to a saint that I would ever get to know and most of all he was a man of honour; he kept his word.

Towards the end of the week we four vin-blonkers boarded the ferry boat at Port Said, our destination was once again Port Fuad and the time was almost midnight. When the ferry boat had reached the middle of the crossing, I was standing by the gunwale gazing down at the foaming water, then suddenly Jimmy Binns whispered into my ear, 'I bet you couldn't swim the rest of the way.'

In a split second, fully clothed and capped I dived from the top of the gunwale and was swimming the fastest hundred yards of my life. As soon as I had judged that I was safely away from the boiling turbulent water created by the thrashing paddles, I stopped swimming, then treading water I turned and gazed back at the chaotic scene aboard the ferry boat. By now the boat had stopped and through the utter confusion of waving arms and echoes of ships' sirens screaming across the black waters at the bewitching hour of midnight, I could see the boat had taken a dangerous list to starboard as every soul on it rushed to one side in order to get a good view of my latest stunt.

As I listened I could hear the excited cries from the passengers, 'I can see him, there he is.'

Suddenly I became the centre of attention in the glare of powerful searchlights which zoomed in from all directions. What better time to take my bow? I then held my cap high above the water giving my captive audience a joyous wave. As the roar of the cheers died away I became aware of a fast approaching motorboat. Thinking that this was no time to be picked up by officials, I replaced my cap on my head and made a desperate bid to get free from the searchlights and swim for the shore. Needless to say I didn't stand a hope in hell and within a couple of minutes the launch was upon me. The Suez police paid no attention to my plea to leave me alone to swim back, so there I was fighting their efforts to pull me on board. Using their boat-hooks they seized me under my collar and finally managed to drag me to the side of the boat and pull me out of the water. The long open launch was manned by no fewer than eight policemen who sat two abreast at equidistant intervals throughout the length of the boat. As I gazed along the boat from my position in the bows, I was thinking how smart they looked in their long white robes and red fez hats, and much to my surprise they all seemed so good-humoured despite my antics. It wasn't until years later that it occurred to me that they thought it was a suicide bid, had they known that it was just a prank I am sure that they would not have released me into the charge of my crew-mates who by now had reached the other side.

After the police had withdrawn from the scene, I grinned at Jimmy Binns who was chuckling all over his chops. 'You mad sod,' he gasped, then added, 'what did you do that for, I was only kidding?'

'Oh well, everybody seemed to enjoy themselves and it did round off the evening,' I answered.

Later while sitting in the mess removing my squelching shoes and sodden clothes, I listened with glee as my evening's associates described the whole episode to the rest of my mess-mates, who by now were rapidly warming their hearts towards me. Needless to say I was enjoying every moment of it. The next morning I woke up at about 0600 hours and immediately thought of my wet clothes which I had left strewn all round the mess-deck, then as I glanced at my cap and once white number six suit which was now covered with oil, it all looked in a right mess. My mind flashed back to what Joe Grisdale had said a few months earlier, 'You don't need much money, but you do need tons of kit.' It was certainly true in my case. I had absolutely nothing left to go ashore in and I think I must have spent four hours that morning scrubbing my white suit and pressing my cap and shoes into some sort of shape in order to go ashore that night.

About that time, Chief Stoker Lee left the boat to return to the UK. To replace him our stoker, PO Thomas, was promoted to chief. This left a vacancy for a stoker PO which was occupied by a new character who answered to the name of Curtain. On reflection he wasn't a bad sort of guy, but at the time I couldn't stand him. To me he seemed an awful show-off and he was a taff, which didn't help things along as far as I was concerned. No matter what subject we discussed he was the expert – he knew it all. It was 0900 in the morning when the conversation turned to water sports and as soon as diving was mentioned Taff started bragging. The boat had only just come off the floating dock and we were moored up to a buoy about a hundred yards away.

Not being able to take any more of Taff's bragging I said to him, 'If you dive from the top of the control tower on the floating dock over there, I will give you my tot.'

'Kiddo you're on,' he answered.

Then as he withdrew from the mess Geordie Heddon looked at me and said, 'Tom you know you have lost your tot.'

'He won't have the guts to do that,' I answered.

Then grinning all over his chops Geordie said, 'Sorry Tom, that is one thing that I know he can do. He is a champion diver.'

At that moment Taff returned to the mess, he had already changed into his swimming trunks. 'Are you ready Kiddo, come up with me and wave goodbye to your tot.'

God, how I hated his arrogance but along with all the other stokers in the mess I followed him on to the casing. A few minutes later I watched him climb the iron ladder. Taking two steps at a time, he looked as sprightly as a monkey and within a couple of minutes he had reached the top. I looked on with ashen face and disbelief as he threw out his arms in a magnificent swallow dive which would have been worthy of an Olympic gold medal. As Pip Piper appeared with the rum ration, Taff was right on his heels and leaving me no doubt that he had come to claim his prize. As I nervously handed him the precious nectar I stood to one side and summoned every ounce of self-control that I could muster. Surely he was going to offer me 'sippers', I thought to myself. Alas no such favour was forthcoming, instead he started to tantalise me by holding the glass to his lips for long agonising seconds. Much to the amusement of my mess-mates he was really enjoying himself while prolonging my suffering.

The giggling suddenly stopped when I couldn't contain myself any longer, I shouted, 'Don't sod about, drink the bloody stuff if you are going to.'

Then came the bombshell, 'I will tell you what I will do,' said Taff. He paused for a second, then lowering the glass he challenged, 'If you dive off the top you can keep your tot.'

'Now's your chance Tom you can do it,' shouted Geordie Heddon.

'It's all right for you but I can't dive,' I answered. Then

after taking a long look at my tot I made my way towards the after hatch. Being only clad in shorts and sandals I climbed on to the casing, kicked off my footwear and dived over the side. I was soon swimming towards the iron ladder which led to the top of the control tower of the floating dock. When I reached the top I stood in the edge and looked down at the water below. The height must have been thirty-five feet and the thought of what I had to do was terrifying. As I stood there, gazing down I looked towards the boat. There in the foreground of a dozen stokers stood Taff, he was holding the tot high in the air. Being unable to withstand the temptation I lunged forward and departed from my foothold in the most uncertain manner. As I flashed past the steel plates on the side of the dock I can remember thinking how close I was to it and when my head hit the water my skull felt as though I had been struck with a slab of concrete. Half-dazed I finally broke surface and waved to my cheering mess-mates. After I scrambled on to the casing I stood there with my knees knocking like the clappers as Taff handed me my tot.

'Kiddo you have earned it,' he said.

From then on, if Taff had told me that he was the king of Wales I would have believed him.

All too soon it was time to say goodbye to our friends in the RC club but not before we vin-blonkers had organised a ship's dance. It was our intention to give all the profits from the sale of the tickets to the club, but the monks wouldn't hear of it, so instead the money was given to Mrs Maxwell who used it to give us winos a sumptuous meal in her private home which was a fine large house, overshadowed by the cathedral. When we arrived at the foot of the steps which led up to the entrance, we were greeted by Mrs Maxwell and her eighteen year old daughter, who with her good looks and charm spiced the evening with romantic aspirations for six lonely sailors. Throughout the evening,

Yvonne gracefully endured the fierce competition as each of us in turn would try to win her attention. With her charisma, I had the feeling that our stations were poles apart and for us sailors she remained as untouchable as a Greek goddess floating by in the clouds.

Meanwhile back in Alexandria, mother *Medway*'s recent losses of submarines *Regulus* and *Triton* was reason enough for *Parthian*'s premature departure from the refit yard in Port Said. Although many major repairs had been completed, it had only been a patch-up job which barely made us seaworthy for another patrol. As soon as the *Parthian* was tied up alongside the *Medway* I was overjoyed to see my old pal Chippy come prancing through the engine room greeting me with the splendid news that he was joining our boat. I couldn't believe my luck it was wonderful to be united again. Ever since we had joined up we had been the best of friends, if one of us was broke then so was the other.

That night when we were celebrating ashore, he told me that Ruck-Keene (Captain 'S'), had sent for him that afternoon. Ruck-Keene had told him, 'I have just received a letter from your father and he is most concerned about your welfare and has asked me to persuade you to write to him, although I cannot compel you to write I sincerely hope that you will do so.' Who could be more qualified to consider a father's feelings of anxiety towards a son's well being in a wartime submarine? He too had a son serving aboard the famous *Upholder* which was commanded by Lieutenant Wanklyn VC.

During the course of the evening I met a few of my old mess-mates off the *Tetrarch*. They told me about a frightening experience they had endured during their last patrol. Their new captain who had previously commanded one of the old 'P' class submarines, while surface running on the *Tetrarch* tried to trim down using an unorthodox method sometimes practised on the 'P' class. This experiment might have had disastrous consequences but for the smart reflexes of Stoker Bell who slammed shut the lower conning tower hatch as the boat suddenly took a deep plunge. Fortunately the boat was quickly blown to the surface where the captain and the five lookouts were picked out of the water, none the worse for their unexpected dip.

Chippy's destiny was decided the next morning when instead of joining the *Parthian* he was drafted to the *Perseus* which had just rejoined the *Medway* after an extensive refit in Malta. Sadly the run ashore that we had the night before was to be the last time that we would drink together. At 1800 hours the following day the *Parthian* slipped through the boom defences at Alexandria. Once again we were heading towards the toe of Italy. Confronted with an eight hundred mile trip it was inevitable that most of our run would be made on the surface. Our guardian angel in the form of atrocious weather protected us from the eyes of enemy aircraft. The climax of that patrol happened on 16th March.

While we were patrolling Italy's southern coastline off Palmi, our captain attacked and sank a supply ship of 3,141 tons. During the depth-charging that followed our after planes jammed again and as the boat had taken a steep stern-down angle I was faced with the same task that befell Stoker Shepherd during our previous patrol. Owing to the fact that he had left the boat to go home, I had inherited his job in the after-ends. With the enemy right above us, so much grease had been used to try and quieten the screeching shaft, that the large master nut used to tighten the stern glands became buried in it. Because of the excess depth, water was pouring through the glands at a frightening rate and with the angle of the trim, the water from the forward bilge had flowed aft and covered the nut completely. Up past my knees in water I reached behind me to grab a handful of cotton waste so that I could wipe the nut clean.

As I did so, the turning shaft whisked the waste from my hand and was gradually being pulled into the glands. Realising that the whole thing might seize, I knew something had to be done quickly. I grabbed the huge spanner and started to hack away at the waste as it spun round the shaft. Suddenly the jaws of the spanner became entangled in the cotton mesh and was snatched from my grip. In a flash the massive steel missile was sent flying over my stooping shoulders, narrowly missing my skull as it crashed thunderously against the steel deck-head just inches above me. Hardly realising how near I had come to grief I reclaimed the spanner and tried the second time. This time I was successful in hacking away the offending waste. Then having done so I stood with one foot on the deck and the other on the grease drum. As I leaned over in order to get a good pull on the spanner, my bent knee started to shake in a most uncontrollable manner as depth-charges exploded just outside the hull above me. The only thing that I could think of at the time, was that it was a blessing that there was no one around to witness my failing nerves.

It takes little imagination to realise that men living in such close contact with each other soon get to know each other's shortcomings as well as their good points. The very nature of a captain's life in a submarine in many respects condemns him to a life of loneliness, but even so, he cannot escape the scrutiny of his crew. Commander Rimmington was no exception. Once at sea he would accept nothing less than first rate efficiency and those that fell short of his expectations he would bear down on like a ton of bricks, in such moods he could be a right tartar. Due to these occasional outbursts he became known to his crew as Von Rimmington, but never within his hearing. Therefore it's quite obvious that we submariners held the German U-boat commanders in high esteem as first rate disciplinarians. Although there were very few of us who hadn't been dragged over the coals sometime or other, we had the sense to realise that it was all for our own good and our lives were in very safe hands. Von also knew that there was a wrong time to chastise a man for making a slip-up. I never once saw him go for anybody during an attack.

Quite often Von would break the monotony of a long day's dive by making a sudden descent from his cabin which was built into the conning tower. As soon as his khaki shorts appeared below the lower hatch the usual chatter in the control room would be reduced to a nervous silence with each of the watchkeepers wondering who would be the target of the day. More often than not it would be Able-Seaman Bell who was endowed with a huge fat belly which was supported by the tops of his thighs as he would sit with his feet apart while operating the big wheel controlling the after hydroplanes. Being equipped with a sense of humour that even Von couldn't quell, he became the perfect victim. On the other hand it could have been Stoker Binns's turn who, unlike Dinger Bell, took everything in life seriously, especially his job which was raising and lowering the periscope. Providing it wasn't you on the end of the captain's derisive yet humorous taunts these antics would often give rise to muffled laughs and sniggers among the remaining watchkeepers. Possibly it was the captain's way of relieving the tension but whatever the reason there was not one man in the crew that didn't admire and respect him.

It was mid-April before we returned to Alexandria and once again we were directed to Port Said for repairs. It was during this short trip when there was some confusion in the control room. After a couple of fruitless attempts to take a sun shot, the captain returned to the chart desk endeavouring to isolate the error on the chart. It had become quite obvious that the navigator had fallen out of favour with the captain who was by that time doing his nut with him. We could have only been a few miles off Port Said yet we were well and truly lost in a thick fog. The whole situation seemed so ridiculous that Pip Piper couldn't resist asking the navigator, 'Where are we now, sir?'

But the question did not embarrass the officer at all. Instead he came back with the answer, 'According to the stars and my navigating we are now fifty miles inside the Libyan desert.'

His flippant reply resulted in a burst of laughter among the control room watchkeepers, but not so the captain who at that precise moment had just returned to the control room. Oh boy! did he tear him off a strip.

After the refit we returned to Alexandria to take in stores and prepare for another patrol. We now had three new faces in the mess and for each one of them it was their first patrol. The three staid men that they relieved were by name Stokers Tate, Jones, and Davies, although I did appreciate the fact that they had been away from the UK for a lot longer than myself, I did feel a little envious about them going home. During the afternoon prior to our evening departure the above events had left me in an unsettled frame of mind and thinking of home. Before leaving I decided to write a few letters. This for me was always an arduous task, so in order to devote my entire concentration to the subject, I took my writing gear along to one of the vacant submarine messes at the stern of the *Medway*. I hadn't been sitting there long before I was disturbed by the crashing and banging of locker doors. As I looked in the direction of the noise I watched a chief PO and a leading seaman remove all the kits from the lockers. Such was the routine after a boat was reported missing. At that time this was becoming an everyday scene aboard the *Medway*, so much so, that I did not bother to find out which boat it was that was overdue.

Instead of showing concern for my unfortunate fellow

submariners, my mind started to dwell on my own situation and thinking that it would only be a matter of time before my own kit would be listed. With these sombre thoughts in mind I returned my uncompleted letter to my locker and went back to my own mess to join in a game of cards. In less than two hours we would be called to harbour stations, so this was no time to be thinking about dying. Owing to three more senior stokers leaving the boat I was elevated to keeping a watch on the diving panel. By that time I had already gained a thorough knowledge of the HP air line so I was able to set about my job with full confidence. During my watch on the third night at sea I had the opportunity to peep over the navigator's shoulder and take a crafty look at the chart. From my observations I was able to deduce that we were about to round Rhodes Island and head towards the Aegean Sea. From little bits of information which was fed to us from time to time together with a certain amount of guesswork, we were pretty certain that our main patrolling area would be somewhere in the region of the Dardanelles.

I had at that time retained only a limited store of knowledge about our submarines' exploits in the Dardanelles area during the First World War but it was enough to confirm my expectations that we had embarked on a hazardous patrol. To get to our patrolling area we had to feel our way through minefields. There was also the hazard of skirting the numerous enemy-occupied islands, and sneaking through the narrow channels which separated them. As we headed towards the first of these islands it seemed that all nature's elements had formed together in the most harmonious setting that could well inspire the imaginative dreams of the romantic author, but for a submariner on a wartime patrol the starry skies, together with a full moon reflecting on a balmy sea, means danger.

During my watch on the diving panel the captain remained on the bridge while a few of the lads were in the process of ditching the gash over the side. This nightly ritual took place round about midnight. Usually a stoker would volunteer to take up a position on the bridge, understandably his job kept him confined to the after-ends or the engine room so this would be his only chance to fill his lungs with fresh air and take a quick look at the sky. The main function of a submarine is to see and not be seen, so for obvious reasons speed of the operation was the essence. The instant the stoker arrived on the bridge, he would lower the rope to his opposite number in the control room, then in quick succession he would hook a bucket of garbage to the ropes end, leaving the man on the bridge to haul it up and hastily dispose of its contents over the side. After a few minutes the chore was complete and the stoker up top would then return to the control room below. On that occasion when his feet touched the deck he remarked, 'I have never seen it so bright before, it's like bloody daylight up there.'

As the gentle roll of the boat responded to the slight swell on the sea I turned about and looked up at the sky through the conning-tower hatch. It was as the man said, as bright as day. As I stood gazing upwards I became fascinated by the scene above me, the orifice of the upper hatch appeared as a circular stage with the distant stars flitting to and fro across the sky simulating the graceful movements of a troupe of ballet dancers. As my mind conjured up such thoughts, I was suddenly brought back to reality as the opening of the conning-tower hatch became completely blocked by fast descending lookouts, at the same moment both telegraphs rang down 'full astern' and almost simultaneously the klaxon sounded for a crash dive. Faults on the telemotor system made it necessary to start the telemotor pump before snapping open the main vents. With the sound of escaping air as the needle on the diving gauge swung to fifty feet I was satisfied that the main vents had opened. At fifty feet the captain gave the order to blow 'Q Tank' then 'shut main vents'. By this time the boat had slipped into a stern dive and although this was something no submariner would relish, our captain was soon able to regain control of the boat and set it on course in a forward direction. During the height of the activity I heard someone in the crew whisper the words, 'Torpedo tracks, they missed us.' It was quite some time before we surfaced again and resumed patrol routine.

By then the next watch had taken over and I went back to the mess feeling quite chuffed with myself, after all it was the first time that I had taken a major part in diving a submarine so perhaps it was not too much for me to expect at least a little cheer from my mess-mates. Full to the brim with conceit I waited for someone to mention the fact but alas they all kept a still tongue and after ten minutes my ego was shattered when not a bloody word was said about it. Still feeling smug I waited until we were all sitting down to breakfast. 'Do you know it was me that dived the boat last night?' I proudly announced.

'So what?' answered Geordie Heddon. Then with a broad grin he added, 'Do you expect to get a bloody medal or something?' Although I joined in the laughter created by his wisecrack, I could have kicked myself for bringing the subject up.

During the watch while submerged, my main duties was to raise or lower the periscope according to the instructions of the officer of the watch or more importantly, the captain. For the first few watches I managed to escape the attention of the latter, but not for long. It was our fifth day on patrol when the captain stood by the after periscope and in a soft voiced ordered 'Up periscope.' Unfortunately for me I did not hear him. So not feeling very pleased with me he turned in my direction and snapped, 'Up periscope.' This time his tone was so much louder that it unnerved me and as the eye piece appeared just above the well-hole I lowered the lever to check its speed of ascent. Then from the captain's hunched position on the deck I tried to control the periscope's smooth rate of travel to correspond with the captain's rising stance. As he waited for me to speed it up he became very impatient and snapped at me once again, 'Up periscope.' By this time I was reduced to a complete bundle of nerves and unintentionally jerked the lever causing the very thing that I had been trying to avoid. The sudden movement of the periscope caught the captain just above his eye.

Half-dazed he glared at me and bellowed, 'I said "Up periscope", not knock my eye out.' As I stood there looking very sorry for myself, he shouted, 'What are you doing there, you are not my periscope watchkeeper?'

Luckily the chief stoker was near at hand and rescued me from my feeble attempt to explain. He told the captain that he was obliged to make changes because of the vacancies caused by the three senior stokers that we left behind in Alexandria. It was obvious to me that the captain was still in a disgruntled mood and I knew that as far as I was concerned there would not be a second chance. Nevertheless for the time being he let the matter drop, but not for long. An hour later the chief stoker informed me that I would no longer be employed in the control room. Instead I was reverted to my old job in the after-ends.

After an uneventful week, excitement grew as the periscope watchkeepers were about to be rewarded for their constant vigilance. They had sighted a convoy of three tankers escorted by an anti-submarine vessel. Three tankers would normally have been a most rewarding target, because the chance of encountering a convoy of this magnitude was very remote. To make the most of this opportunity, our captain was faced with the difficult task of getting close enough to get a good shot at them, but this was never to be, because by hugging the coast in shallow waters the enemy deprived us of a good score. Each time they came within the captain's sight he was foiled by their cunning manoeuvres. It was as if they were aware of our watchful eyes and he just couldn't get a bearing on them. Protected as they were by the shallow waters on one side and the neutral zone not far away it became impossible to deliver a positive shot at all the targets. Given no other alternative he had to settle for firing a salvo from extreme range which only enabled him to score hits on one of the ships, the master of which took evasive action by running it aground before it had time to sink.

Imagine our surprise when it was passed along the grapevine that the escort had turned tail and was quickly making tracks towards the horizon. The Italians' apparent lack of enthusiasm to become involved in the conflict caused bursts of laughter among us in the engine room.

'They are running away,' someone shouted. Unfortunately our smug conceit was far too premature to start rejoicing because within an hour we were on the receiving end of a frenzied depth-charge attack. After several hours we managed to give the destroyers the slip and make for less hostile waters so that we could make good the damage that we had suffered.

During the next few days our captain was showing a keen interest in the island of Lesbos and judging by his careful study of the charts we all knew that something was brewing in his mind. But it was not until we were called to diving stations that we found out what his intentions were. We were told that we were going to proceed through a long narrow channel into a large basin in the centre of the island. Once inside we would do as much damage as we could, before making our escape. We were told that it would be dangerous because the channel was shallow and there was every probability of aircraft attack In the event of things going wrong, we were quite near to neutral territory so there would not be much to worry about if we had to make a dash for it.

Sometime during the forenoon the *Parthian* slowly edged its way up the narrow channel, the sea was dead calm with not so much as a ripple to be seen on the surface which barely covered the bridge. With our keel dragging the seabed, the use of telegraphs was forbidden and all orders to the motor room was passed by word of mouth. As we sat around in small groups the overwhelming silence became eerie. It was always the waiting that seemed more terrifying than the actual event. After a quarter of an hour word was passed aft that we were now inside the basin. After a quick sweep round on the periscope the only targets to be seen were two large schooners which were moored in the centre of the basin and a lighter which was alongside a jetty. Although these craft could be made good use of by the enemy the prize seemed hardly worth exposing the boat to a possible retaliation by shore batteries.

At the time my diving station was in the after-ends and I became excited when word was passed to me that the two stern tubes would be used in the attack. Normally there was never a torpedo operator stationed in the after-ends but all my expectations of being called upon to actually fire the torpedoes was swept from my mind when one of the torpedo men appeared on the scene. In the meantime the captain had turned the boat round in order to make a hasty exit by way of the channel. After a few tense seconds the after tubes indicated 'Fire', and the fish were on their way. The shock waves which followed the explosions almost blew the boat to bits. Somewhat disappointed with the morning's work, word had been passed that one of the torpedoes had sunk the two schooners and the other had wandered all round the harbour and finally hit the jetty and the lighter, and having nothing else to aim at we were soon making haste back down the channel to deep water. Luckily we got there before the alerted air patrols were able to harm us.

A few days had passed before we got near to the end of another successful patrol. As usual the news of our recall had been passed through the boat like a flash of lightning within seconds of it being received. This long-awaited signal was always a tonic which never failed to provide us with a new lease of life at the end of a dreary patrol. This was the time when everyone was up and about and one of the seamen would be sitting in the fore-end engaged in his regular assignment. With the *Parthian*'s Jolly Roger draped across his knees he would be proudly sewing another three bars to our already respectable score. As we came within sight of the boom which protected the entrance to Alexandria Harbour we all knew that it would only be a matter of minutes before we were reading our mail, at least that is what we thought at the time. After being closed up to harbour stations for half an hour or more I began to wonder what on earth was causing the delay.

'We seem to be a long time getting alongside,' I shouted to the chief.

'Yes, I have just sent through to find out what is going on,' he answered.

At that moment one of the stokers returned from the control room shouting, 'The boom is closed and they won't let us through, Von is on the bridge doing his nut.'

With no hint of an explanation the *Parthian* continued to pound backwards and forwards for almost two hours. When eventually we did arrive alongside the *Medway*, we began to hear a whisper that a very young sparker had missed the signal warning us to stay clear of the boom. It seemed that overnight the Italians had mined the same area that we had been ploughing through all the morning!

Shortly after this we experienced another hair-raising episode. While travelling on the surface not far from Alexandria, the lookouts spotted a Catalina anti-submarine patrol flying boat. Realising that the friendly aircraft had already committed themselves by an irreversible decision to attack, the officer took the only evasive option open to him. He dived the boat. No sooner had the lookout's feet hit the deck below than a number of explosions rocked the boat and almost deafened us. As a result of these explosions most of the lights were extinguished and our main batteries sustained severe damage. As the smoke and fumes quickly spread throughout the boat, the almost choking LTO groped around in the dark in frantic efforts to restore emergency lighting and because of the acrid condition below, the captain was forced to surface far sooner than it was otherwise safe to do so. Whether or not the RAF had realised their mistake, I don't know, but thank God they did not return to bomb us again.

Gradually essential repairs were made to the machinery and we were able to return to Alexandria under our own steam. The next day we left Alexandria en route for Port Said where an exchange battery was available to replace our damaged one.

On our arrival the captain cleared lower deck and passed on the following message, 'I have just received a signal from the RAF, they say that they are extremely sorry for mistaking us for the enemy and that they wish to make amends by inviting us to be their guests at their base. Having no wish to be responsible for the outcome of such a meeting I have declined the invitation.'

It was not long before we received a reply to our refusal. The saucy buggers sent us a silver bomb mounted on a polished plaque on which was inscribed the words: 'The Devil Takes Care of His Own.'

Owing to the Italians stepping up their nightly air raids

on our ships in Alexandria harbour, each evening it became customary for all submarines alongside the *Medway* to disperse to different locations within the harbour. One particular night when I was on duty the *Parthian* was directed to a berth alongside the harbour wall, the time was just after midnight soon after I had taken over the middle watch on the casing. Only two nights prior to this the Italian frogmen had penetrated the harbour and managed to blow up one or two of our ships. With this in mind I became quite concerned when I heard some tapping noises coming from the hull. Being uncertain what caused the tapping I went down into the boat and shook the duty PO who then came up top and listened. He in turn called the duty officer who then called the duty signalman and ordered him to flash a signal to the parent ship explaining what was happening. About ten minutes later a motor launch came alongside carrying a gunnery rating equipped with a few five pound depth-charges. The duty officer then told me to inform the duty watch that we were going to drop some five pound depth-charges over the side and to advise them to present themselves on the casing forthwith. The only thanks that I got from my sleeping shipmates was a whole string of abuse which when deciphered simply meant they were not the least bit worried about a few five pound depth-charges so they stayed in their bunks. Seconds after the first explosion I had never before seen such panic, they poured from the hatches like swarming bees, they had not taken into account that the boat was alongside the wall thus shaking its hull more severely than it otherwise would have done. They didn't think it was a bit funny when those that were wise enough to come up top were doubled up laughing. By the time we discovered that it was the mooring springs that were tapping the hull it was time for my relief to take over the watch and as he did so I could see that he wasn't a bit happy.

'I suppose you are now going to get your head down now that you have kept all of us awake half the night,' he said.

On 25th June, 1941, the *Parthian* was proceeding on the surface trim down at a moderate speed just outside Beirut, and just before midnight our captain was called to the bridge when just a mere speck of a craft was seen on the horizon. When we closed in he was able to identify the craft as that of a large ocean-going French submarine, two of which were thought to be under the Vichy influence and were a threat to allied shipping while operating from Beirut. Catching them completely unaware Commander Rimmington was able to get close enough to deliver the fatal blow using a salvo of six torpedoes. Although the orders were to attack and sink the boat, because of it being one of our own kind the crews' feeling about the encounter was one of remorse and the most sensitive and least satisfying of all our engagements. Such was our view that we did not add a bar to our Jolly Roger. Having said this I hasten to add that but for the sharp eyes of our lookouts the fate of the two submarines could have well been reversed.

Soon after our return to *Alexandria*, we received the news that the *Parthian* was returning to the UK for a much needed overhaul. Although most of her crew had been with her since she left China a year earlier, there were a few of us who had joined the boat since. As expected these men were taken off and replaced by men who had been away for two years or more. I had been on the *Parthian* for all but one of her wartime patrols so I was not surprised when I remained with her almost to the last minute. Firmly believing that I would be going home with her, I was absolutely shattered when I was told that I would be drafted to the spare crew to make way for another stoker who had only just arrived on the station and was already being sent home on compassionate grounds. Feeling thoroughly dejected I said goodbye to the happiest crew that I had ever sailed with.

Sometime during November 1941, I was sitting in *Medway*'s spare crew mess when I was overjoyed to hear that the *Perseus* was expected alongside at 1800 hours. Two months before she left *Medway* bound for Malta, so I was very much looking forward to being reunited with my pal, Chippy. Having changed into my number 1s, I was all set to leave for shore as soon as Chippy was ready to join me. However half an hour had passed and still no sign of the *Perseus*. After supper I was becoming very fidgety and puzzled because of the boat's late arrival.

'What could be the reason for the boat's delay?' I was asking my fellow mess-mates.

Another half hour had passed when a pipe over the tannoy announced, 'Tombola is now being played on the fore-well deck.' Being tired of hanging about waiting I went up to join in the games which kept me occupied for another hour. With the games now over the time was 2000 hours and still no sign of Chippy, so I now settled down to watch a film being showed on the fore-well deck. In the meantime all kinds of rumours was being passed along the grapevine.

At the time all of us in the spare-crew mess were quite convinced that *Medway* had received the *Perseus*'s ETA. Soon after 2200 hours when the film operator shut down for the night I decided that it was too late to think about shore leave now so I spread my hammock out on the mess-deck table with the idea of going to sleep for the night. I then became conscious of continuous distant explosions. Surely it wasn't the *Perseus* being mistakenly depth-charged outside of the harbour, I wondered. After a long time I did manage to go to get to sleep. The following day there were strong rumours that the Destroyer *Jervice*, had mistaken the *Perseus* for the enemy and sunk it. Today the official view according to the Admiralty is that the *Perseus* was sunk by a mine well away from Alexandria, but I still have my doubts. Fifty years on I met someone who was aboard the *Jervice*. At that time he told me that all of those aboard had accepted the fact that *Jervice* had scored a home goal.

Chapter Seven
Thrasher

It was during the month of June 1941 when the parent ship mother *Medway* was to acquire a substantial increase to her spare crew. My friend Harry Carpenter, 'Chippy', was one of many who had taken passage from the UK via Cape Town, South Africa. Such replacements for tired out and worn down crews were long overdue. A typical example for the need of these replacements can be made clear to all, through the experience of a colleague of mine who was an 'Asdic' operator. He recently told me what had happened to him during those times. While sweeping for HE on a previous patrol, depth-charges had caused damage to one of his ears which started to bleed. On the eve of his next patrol he explained to his captain that because of the trouble it was giving him he was going to report sick and that he would not be sailing with the boat. My friend was somewhat taken by surprise when his captain angrily retorted, 'Good Heavens, man, you've got another ear. Get your things back down in the boat, you are going on patrol.'

Having taken advantage of the opportunity of having a long spell in harbour, I became reconciled to the fact that my Mediterranean patrols were far from finished. I had reasoned with myself that despite the danger, I was always happier in a boat, and up to now I had been extremely lucky in sharing both good and bad times with the type of men that I had been privileged to call shipmates. On the other hand the mundane routine of life on the parent ship HMS *Medway* was not all that I had imagined.

With these thoughts in mind together with grieving over the loss of my friend Chippy I asked to be drafted to one of the newcomers to the Mediterranean, namely the s/m *Thrasher*. Although she had a dismal record to date as the result of her first few patrols, she was now under new command, that of Lieutenant HE MacKenzie. For him and the crew success was immediate. They had just returned from a patrol off Benghazi with a bar sewn to their otherwise bare Jolly Roger. That bar represented one supply ship which they had torpedoed and sunk on 28th October, 1941. This was to start a long run of successful operations most of which I, as a new member of the crew, was to witness.

Thrasher's next patrol was also a success when yet another of our torpedoes found its mark in the centre of a supply ship of 3,510 tons. This sinking was of special significance because we managed to penetrate the entrance to the Adriatic and score what must have been a demoralising blow to the enemy's defence of their own backyard. No longer would the port of Brindisi be considered a safe haven for Italian ships to go to and fro.

Apart from the *Tetrarch* I don't think any of our submarines had managed to venture so far into the Adriatic for over twelve months, when the *Regent* almost dropped a clanger when she broke surface in the middle of the Italian fleet. After returning to Alexandria, damage to our batteries caused by depth-charges made it necessary for us to proceed through the canal and down to Suez so that we could replace the broken cells with new ones. It wasn't much of a place to spend Christmas, but it was far better than being on patrol and we were soon to discover that our anticipated misery did have a happy ending. This came about when Father Christmas left forty-eight thousand crates of bottled beer almost on our doorstep. Of course he didn't exactly inform us that it was put there to ensure our well being. The existence of the stash was made known to me on the first evening of my arrival. It was during a visit to a makeshift canteen in the dockyard. The place was nothing more exciting than a small hut where one could buy a carton of canned beer which was served through a small cubby hole in the corner. After a few drinks I began to get on friendly terms with a couple of soldiers who were sitting near by. After sharing a few drinks they told me not to buy any more because there was plenty of it outside in the dockyard.

'It was with the cargo which was salvaged from the liner *Ceorgic* when it was bombed,' they said. When I told them that it was probably under guard they told me not to worry about it because they were the guards. 'You can all help yourselves,' they said.

Needing no second invitation I hurried back to the boat to spread the good news. The rest of that evening was spent stocking up by all and sundry. There were drinks galore for evermore. The booze, together with two large turkeys to share between fifteen stokers, were all the ingredients needed to celebrate the Christmas festival. One pleasant surprise happened during the forenoon on Christmas day. The time was just after eleven, the bewitching hour of tot time. Who should step into the mess? None other than the captain himself.

With a warm smile on his face he greeted us, 'A merry Christmas everybody, have you got everything that you need?'

Some understatement that was! There was beer all over the bloody place. Having never seen the captain before that morning, his presence was indeed an unexpected pleasure which delighted all of us. Never before had I seen a captain show so much concern for the welfare of his crew.

I was not alone with these thoughts because the Stoker's

response was overwhelming when a chorus of voices rang out, 'Everything is fine, a merry Christmas to you, sir.'

'Now that you are here you must sit down and drink a tot with us,' one of the leading hands insisted.

To see him take a seat between us as we surrounded the mess table, gave us a tremendous amount of pleasure.

When I reminded him about it quite recently he replied, 'Oh yes, I remember it quite well, but what you didn't know was that I was waylaid by the members of the other three messes, and having to please you all it ruined my appetite for an important dinner that I had been invited to attend.'

During the early part of January our next patrol took us into the Ionian Sea where we added a third bar to our Jolly Roger by sinking another ship of 5,016 tons. As with each of the previous assaults, the attacks were always punished with a bombardment of depth-charges. We never got anything for free. I suppose in a way it relieved our conscience of any guilt that we may have felt.

On Friday morning, 13th February, 1942, the task of taking on provisions for our next patrol was near to completion, when the tannoy summoned all hands to muster in the fore-ends. At the time there had been whispers throughout the boat that we would not be going out until the next day. Whether or not the captain got to hear about these rumours I don't know, but this is what happened. I suppose all sailors have superstitions of one kind or another but the captain nipped them in the bud when he had all hands gathered in the fore-ends eagerly awaiting to hear what he had to say. A few of us at the front shuffled back to make room for the captain to use the fore-end ladder as a vantage point from which he could address us. The ship's company having previously being called to attention by the coxswain, we watched our commanding officer climb a few rungs up, then turning round to face us he said, 'Ship's company at ease. I suspect that some of you feel a little apprehensive about proceeding on patrol today because Friday 13th is considered to be unlucky. Of course it's unlucky, but not for us – for the enemy,' he stressed.

At dusk the same evening our boat slipped pass the open boom which guarded the harbour. This time our patrolling area was to be the shipping lanes in and out of Crete. This will be one of the easier patrols I thought. How wrong I was. It was about 0900 on the morning of February 16th when the captain was called to the control room. The officer on periscope watch had sighted a promising target on the horizon. I say promising because of the fact that it was heavily escorted by a most up-to-date anti-submarine vessel and what was most unusual was the presence of a lone plane which was engaged in taking long sweeps of the surrounding sea which at the time had a surface as smooth as clear glass. Any tell-tale tracks like that of a feathered wake which would certainly trail behind a moving periscope, would stand out like a sore thumb. To get within range to make a successful torpedo attack would be a very tricky operation indeed. Full marks to our captain who measured up to the challenge. It was a calculated risk which did pay off in the end.

With both main motors 'Slow ahead' together, Thrasher moved stealthily towards the unsuspecting target. Should our presence be discovered before a successful strike our hopes of escape would be very small. With no worries about picking up survivors the heavy escort would have nothing to deter them from launching their full venom upon us. But thanks to Mac, such worries were partially minimised when he scored direct hits on the vessel. In doing so he must have caused a slight hesitation before the enemy reacted. In turn our captain took advantage of the vital seconds lost by them and altered course with both main motors 'grouped up, full ahead'. But not before the plane had seen the torpedo tracks and dropped a marker to pinpoint our position. The dull thud of exploding torpedoes was overwhelmed by the thunderous noise of exploding bombs as a stick of them straddled our boat. Almost immediately came the sound of racing screws screaming towards us and we barely reached a depth of two hundred feet before a multitude of depth-charges came raining down on us. The violent explosions caused failure to the lighting and damage to depth gauges not to mention the sheer terror that we the entombed had to endure, but such was the fortune of all submariners who served in wartime.

It was well into the evening before we dared to hope that the tactics employed by the captain had gradually shaken off the escort vessels whose exploding depth-charges were still faintly heard in the distance. But by that time we had something else to worry about, because when we reached the open sea which by then had become quite turbulent thus causing the boat to roll from side to side each time she came to periscope depth. As she did so continual loud clanking bangs echoed throughout the boat. It took little imagination to realise that an unexploded bomb was rolling to and fro across the hull. For us inside it, thoughts that each bang could trigger off an explosion was a terrifying experience that we had to suffer, but as the evening went on I managed to reconcile myself by surrendering my fate to the laps of the gods. As I became more used to the banging my mind became oblivious to the impending danger and was able to turn over in my bunk and go to sleep. It was about midnight when I woke up with a start.

'What the hell is going on?' I asked myself. I was deafened by the sound of the boat's screws which were just below my bunk, they were thrashing away like the clappers. As I suddenly realised that the boat was going 'full astern, group up', my mind flashed back to my experience during a

Parthian patrol when we evaded a salvo of six torpedoes that the Italians had fired at us. Was the same thing happening again? My fears were worsened when I looked round to discover that there wasn't a soul in sight and as I shot out of my bunk and raced towards the motor room I was convinced that I was the only one left on the boat. It was a great relief to find at least the watchkeepers remained at their posts.

'What's happening, Lou?' I asked the motor room operator.

'It's all right now, it's all over. They have just lowered two bombs over the bows in a sack,' he shouted back.

It wasn't until my mess-mates returned to the mess that I became aware of just how lucky we had been as one of the bombs had made a gaping hole in the steel structure surrounding the bridge and had come to rest under the gun platform. The other one was found in a precarious position lying on top of the steel casing half way between the bows and the gun-tower. Had it just tipped over the edge it would have gone crashing into the saddle tanks sending us all to kingdom come.

A week or so later we lay in dock in Port Said when suddenly I heard a click on the tannoy and the sound of the coxswain's voice. 'All hands to muster on the quayside.'

Being eager to find out what was going on I hastened towards the gangway then reaching the dockside I joined the rest of the crew who had already been marshalled into two ranks. For a minute or two we stood in silence while waiting for the captain to address us. When doing so he read out loud from a document held in his hand the following citation. From memory it was worded roughly as follows:

Although *Thrasher* was still being hunted by the enemy it was necessary for me to dispose of the bombs.

I ordered Lieutenant Roberts and Petty Officer Gould to crawl through the casing and climb through to free the bomb from the obstruction beneath the gun-tower and bring it on top of the casing. Then they had to lower both bombs over the bow, both men knowing full well what I would have to do should the enemy intervene, but did not hesitate to obey my orders.

Having spent three weeks in the dock *Thrasher* was recalled to Alexandria where she lay alongside the *Medway* taking in stores and fuel for our next patrol. This time we were destined for the Cyrenaican Coast somewhere off Benghazi. Once again the sinking of two ships 2,326 tons each added to *Thrasher*'s successful run of patrols. Unfortunately fate wasn't so kind to another of our submarines. When we arrived back in Alexandria we were informed that the famous *Upholder* had been lost just a few miles along the coast from where we were patrolling off Benghazi. I could recall hearing numerous explosions in the distance but I had no idea at the time that it was the end of an exceptional run of successes for the brave captain and crew of the small but famous submarine *Upholder*. Lieutenant Commander David Wanklyn, their captain, had just been awarded the Victoria Cross.

It was early in May 1942 when I boarded the *Thrasher* to start what was to be my last wartime patrol in the Mediterranean. This time we were bound for the dreaded Adriatic Sea. After days of searching for a suitable target the captain's patience was finally rewarded. The twilight of the evening was giving way to darkness when a ship of 1,160 tons loomed over the horizon. As the captain closed in to start the attack he could faintly distinguish the flag flying from its mast, it was the Swastika and further scrutiny disclosed that it was carrying troops. Despite this, war is war and

145

there was no room for sentiment. Like all other enemy ships that came within sight of *Thrasher's* periscope lens, it was destined to find its way to the bottom of the ocean.

Soon after, we received the *Thrasher's* recall to our base in Alexandria. Within minutes of our arrival alongside the *Medway* I heard a whisper that I would soon be returning to the UK.

Chapter Eight

The *Medway* and Otus

On 27th June, 1942, Leading Stoker Hart and myself received the glad tidings that we were to be drafted to the *Medway* to await passage back to the UK. We were both given the option to remain on the *Thrasher* and do one more patrol, after which time she herself was expected to return to home waters. Despite the efforts of our crew-mates to persuade us to remain with them, we declined the offer. Perhaps this was not so surprising because fresh in our minds were the sad thoughts of our last farewell to Topsy Turner who, like us had been away from home for two and a half years, yet only a short while before had been drafted to the *Triumph* to do an extra patrol. Topsy had previously served on the *Parthian* with me. Once, during a morbid conversation about the number of boats that failed to return, he had said to me, 'Stick with me kid and you will see the end of this war.' Ironically the look on his face as he said his last farewell showed no sign of such optimism on that day. His countenance was black. It was as if he knew that this was the end.

Obviously feeling very distraught he had said to Hart and me, 'It's all right for you two to chuckle, you will both be going home in a couple of days.'

Then as he walked down the gangway we both jokingly shouted after him, 'Stop your beefing and get on with it.' We did not know then that he would never return from that patrol.

For a few days Sid Hart better known to his friends as Sam, happily passed the evenings playing tombola or watching films on the *Medway*'s fore-well deck. One such evening found Sam and I in a restless mood, the suspense of knowing that we were going home, but not knowing when, put us in a fidgety frame of mind. To relieve the stress we found ourselves sauntering towards the parent ship's massive recreation space. Such comfortable surroundings would at least provide us with a snug seat whilst we listened to the radio. As usual the place was buzzing with the familiar chatter of boats' crews and the *Medway*'s ship's company We arrived at the scene just in time to hear the chimes of Big Ben's vibrating tones which in those days seemed to electrify the whole atmosphere, so often being the prelude to dismal news about allied losses. The air raids at home were a terrible worry to us, but even more distressing to us submariners was the ever-increasing number of departed friends who had the misfortune to be serving on the ill-fated boats that were lost on patrol.

As the echoes of the last chimes died away we listened to the announcement: 'This is the BBC from London. The Victoria Cross has been awarded to Lieutenant Roberts and Petty Officer Gould of the submarine *Thrasher*.'

The commentator then went on to give a detailed account of everything that had happened in Suda Bay, Crete. Then for a brief second there was deadly silence, then suddenly the news that followed was drowned by the roaring cheers which were almost deafening. Open-mouthed, Sam and I looked at each other as if to reassure ourselves that we were not dreaming. We knew that they would receive some recognition for their bravery, but for two Victoria Crosses to be awarded to our recent shipmates made us feel very proud.

Soon after, Sam and I became aware of rapid changes

which were taking place in Alexandria. First of, all the expected departure of the submarine *Otus* to the UK was cancelled. For Sam and me that was bad news, but there was worse to follow. Instead of boarding her to take passage home I found myself fitted out with a tin hat and gaiters and before I had time to realise what was happening I was in the company of a hundred other sailors all of whom were equally puzzled as myself as to what the Navy intended to do with us. Soon we were all being herded into canvas-covered trucks all pointing towards the battle front of El Alamein. As the convoy sped towards the outskirts of Alexandria I asked my fellow travellers if they knew where we were going but their negative replies only created further speculation in my bewildered mind. Surely they didn't expect us trained submariners to be able to adapt ourselves to desert warfare? As I stood trying to keep my foothold in the swerving truck I kept a constant watch on the dusty road falling behind us. Hindered by the swerving bodies of taller sailors I managed to crane my neck in time to get a fleeting glimpse of long a column of army wagons. Each of these were laden with what I judged to be battle fatigued troops who were soon to be hospitalised in Alexandria and left to the tender care of beautiful nurses. Meanwhile I could only imagine the army in full retreat leaving a handful of we unlikely warriors to take on Rommel's mighty force in a rearguard action. What crazy loon had dreamed up this idea? I thought.

With all this in mind I suddenly became aware that our truck had veered off the dusty road and was coming to a halt inside a wire enclosure. Having jumped off the back of the truck I made a quick survey of my surroundings and came to the conclusion that the place was a storage dump. Thinking that I had solved the answer to our mystery mission I began to wonder how would one go about blowing this lot up. Very soon any notion I had about playing with gun powder was terminated. As I stood looking towards the front of the column my attention was drawn to the antics of the martial, who in the haste that one might have expected from a terrified matador in full retreat with an angry bull at his heels, came running towards us shouting, 'Go back to your trucks.' Then making a circular gesture with his hands, he added, 'Report back to wherever you came from.' It was early the same evening before we very reluctant desert fighters returned to *Medway*.

During the day the ship had left its moorings in the centre of the harbour and was now tied up alongside the dockyard wharf. One glance at the fore-well deck explained the reason why. She was fully laden with a hundred or more torpedoes and diverse spares which had been scattered about the various sheds in the dockyard. As I stepped off the gangway on to the fore-well deck it was as if it was a signal for the crane operator to spring into action by lowering the jib towards the slings which harnessed the gangway and by the time I reached my mess the ship was under way.

Although I was not officially one of the *Medway*'s ship's company, I was detailed to keep watch below with my first stint commencing at midnight. After breakfast the next morning when all hands had completed their mess cleaning chores, a few of us decided to take advantage of a beautiful sunny morning by airing ourselves on the fo'c'sle. As I sauntered forward by the way of the ship's company messes it struck me how casual and carefree everybody was; the whole atmosphere seemed that of a peacetime cruise with the war a million miles away. When we arrived at our chosen spot on the port side of the fo'c'sle we joined a few others among whom was my old pal and shipmate, Sam. I moved over to where he was standing near to the guard-rail, then for a few seconds I stood silently in thought while I was admiring our formidable escort of two cruisers and three destroyers.

'Isn't the sea calm?' someone remarked.

'It's just right for a swim,' I answered. Almost simultaneously with my words came three successive gigantic explosions which shook our massive floating factory with all the violence of an erupting volcano. Not expecting a submarine attack so far east in the Mediterranean my first reaction was to search the sky for bombers. As the ship took a heavy list to starboard, we on the fo'c'sle stood motionless. With what must have been three gaping wounds in her side it was as if mother *Medway* was in agony as repeated short blasts from her siren announced the urgency of her situation. Already our escort had dispersed from its position on our port flank and it was making full speed towards the estimated position of the attacking submarine and at any second was about to launch what proved to be a frenzied depth-charge attack because moments later the whole ocean around us became a massive boiling stew pot as thousands of tons of it spewed up from the depths below as a result of the explosions.

Below where I was standing, the sound of crashing crates brought my attention to the scene on the fore-well deck where a sudden lurch to starboard had caused an avalanche of sliding packed torpedoes. These crates had previously been stacked from six to eight high but very soon most were lost to the mercy of the sea and had anybody been in their path they would have known very little about it Looking back to the port side I caught sight of our chief crusher, or more correctly, Chief Regulating Petty Officer Penfold. With the starboard side of this giant ship already awash the port side had risen to twice its normal height out of the water. Realising this, the well-respected chief was hastily cutting long lengths from a new coil of rope and tying it to the guard-rail so as to enable the reluctant divers to clamber down into the sea. No doubt his action did save a few lives but at the inevitable cost of a large number of rope-burned hands. To date I had been on the dispatch end of torpedoes no fewer than twenty times, but this was the other side of the coin. It was only then that I realised the full extent of a submarine's powers of destruction. It was as though I was looking down from a viewpoint in another world while my whole being became numb with disbelief of the actual events.

Within five minutes from the first explosion a voice behind me uttered the words, 'Mother *Medway* has had it.' It was then when I looked up at the bridge only to find that Captain Ruck-Keene had also reconciled himself to the ship's fate. 'Abandon ship,' he ordered. By then most of my companions had departed. It was my guess that they had chosen the lowest point to leave the ship as understandably they did not relish such a high dive from the fo'c'sle where the height from the water line was increasing with every passing second.

Considering my own options I waited for a few minutes observing everything that was going on around me and as I did my eyes focused towards the boat-deck which was about twenty-five yards away on the opposite side of the fore-well deck. The nearest boat to me was in the process of being lowered when suddenly one end of it dropped into the sea while at the same time ejecting all its occupants in a forward thrust towards the bow.

Immediately after I caught sight of another close friend who like me was always ready for a laugh. Even at a time like that Paddy Boyle was not about to let us down. High up on the boat-deck he stood poised to leap forward and grab hold of an inviting rope which was dangling into the sea, then having done so the massive spool which housed the rope began spin round like a top, while seemingly Paddy was having great fun as he fought to free himself from the mass of coiled rope around his body.

Having no wish to take part in such frolics I decided to keep well away from the scene and chance a high dive off the fo'c'sle. Taking my last look at the bridge I heard the captain shout to the signalman, 'Signal stop depth-charging.' Then for the second time that year my skull felt as though it had been hit by a boulder having taken the highest dive of my life. Being a strong swimmer myself it didn't occur to me that there may be others less capable. By that time the ship was sinking fast and my only thoughts were to put as much distance as possible between me and the swirling vortex. It took a few minutes before the signal to stop depth-charging was put into operation, in the meantime my system became sickened by the shock waves of the distant explosions.

When I reached a distance which I judged to be safe from the suction of the sinking ship I turned to look back on the scene of destruction. Thirty yards behind me a large number of heads were bobbing up and down in the swell and the only part of the *Medway* which remained visible was her bows. In sad defiance of her inevitable fate she sat motionless with her remains glistening under the brilliant sun. I looked on in horror as a solitary figure garbed in a white shirt and trousers struggled to keep his foothold on the ever-increasing slope of the deck.

'Why doesn't he jump for it?' I asked myself. During that time the destroyer *Zulu* was closing in to pick up survivors and as I swam towards her she suddenly swung stern first towards me. Instantly I became aware of her bearing down on me with her deadly screws thrashing like the clappers. Then for the first time since I entered the water I thought that my life was in danger. In a desperate bid to escape the churning screws I turned tail and swam like mad back towards the main group who were bobbing up and down at least thirty yards behind me. Almost on the verge of exhaustion I turned to look back at the destroyer and to my relief it had come to a standstill.

Anxious to know what the destroyer's next move would be, I remained still as it veered round broadside on to me. After a few strokes I climbed up the mesh mats which the deckhands had rigged on her starboard side. As I set foot on the *Zulu*'s deck, I instinctively turned to take a last look at the *Medway*, she was now poised to take her last plunge into the depths of the ocean and again to my horror the terrified man in white was still clutching to the guard-rail of the *Medway*'s fo'c'sle. Too scared to move or heed our gestures to jump he stood upright waving one arm in the air. Seconds afterwards all that could be seen was a tremendous whirlpool as the gallant lady gave up her last breath. Within ten minutes the *Zulu*'s upper deck was strewn with survivors who sat huddled together in small groups, with silent tongues they all seemed content to sit in thought.

After scouring a sea of floating debris and seeing no more sign of life the search was abandoned. Both telegraphs alerted the chief ERA in the *Zulu*'s engine room to open the throttles. Full speed ahead. For a while I squatted on the *Zulu*'s gun platform just gazing down at the white foam while trying to recapture the morning's events. At the time it seemed that I was in the middle of a dream, and as real as the stark truth was, I was unable to grasp the fact. Soon the heavy spray and the cold sea air began to chill my almost naked body, so seeking to make myself more comfortable I sought refuge and hospitality within the stokers' mess and I was not to be disappointed. Already they had provided a large urn full of tea and were doing their best to console a dozen or so grief-stricken survivors.

Sipping our tea we began to talk about our recent experience. The first of two factors which came under severe criticism was the fact that because of the limited capability of an old Greek supply ship called the *Corinthia*, the speed of the convoy had been restricted to eight knots. Whether or not the three knot deficit would have made any difference to the outcome was perhaps a matter of conjecture but nevertheless the logic behind the strategy employed certainly seemed open to question. Another point that came under discussion was the failure to launch the sea-boats. While some of us thought that the launching apparatus was faulty, others said it was the mishandling by inexperienced hands. From my own observations I suspected the latter.

A click on the *Zulu*'s tannoy, followed by the announcement, 'Up spirits', brought the debate to an end as we raced to get to the front of the queue. After the rum issue I returned to the stokers' mess, but there was no time to pick up the threads of our previous conversation because the tannoy once again demanded our attention. 'All hands to muster aft for the funeral of Chief Petty Officer Penfold.'

For a few seconds I was dumbfounded, 'What the hell happened?' I gasped.

Feeling thoroughly shocked this sad news sickened me as only a couple of hours earlier I had seen him dashing about tying ropes to the handrail. To me it seemed that his only concern was for the safety of his fellow shipmates while giving little heed to his own plight. Among many of his outstanding qualities he was a strong swimmer. 'How could this happen? I wondered. Having reached an open space near the quarterdeck we assembled in a reasonably orderly fashion round the canvas coffin which had been placed on the end of a long plank near the port side. Close to the foot of the coffin the *Zulu*'s captain began to read aloud from an open prayer book while we with bowed bare heads stood motionless, being only conscious of the captain's spoken words and the sound of the swishing waves. As the short service ended with the words, 'We commit his body to the deep,' the coxswain lifted the end of the plank high in the air and as he did so the body slid from under the white ensign and splashed into the sea.

During the day I began to piece together what happened to Penfold. From snippets of conversation among the survivors I discovered that he had last been seen in the water near to the boat that went crashing into the sea. He was seen assisting lesser swimmers and while doing so the boat fell on him, causing the injuries from which he died. Such was a tragic end to a man who had endeared himself to all that knew him. Nobody knew better than I how helpful and understanding this man could be. More than once in the past he had steered me out of trouble.

I can recall one day in particular – it was the day when I first learned about the fate of the *Perseus* and the loss of my dear friend, Chippy. The stress of recent patrols together with this sad news had undermined my ability to behave in a rational manner. For me it was the worst time during the whole war. Never before had my morale sunk to such a low ebb. In an effort to overcome my depression I sought medication during a run ashore in Alexandria. My visits to numerous bars did little to restore my fading courage. Nevertheless it did do something for me. By late evening I had been rendered completely legless, almost speechless, and ten bob to the pound between the ears. Despite these setbacks I managed to find my way back to the quay near to the dockyard gates. As I moved towards the already packed motor launch, a voice shouted, 'Get a move on you are already five minutes late.' On hearing the coxswain's plea I dismissed the idea of using the steps instead I took a running jump and landed in the middle of a crowd who were standing in the stern sheets.

'Cast off, I have arrived,' I shouted. Unfortunately my bruised companions were not amused and if threats were anything to go by I would be dead by the following day. It was almost midnight when the boat pulled alongside the *Medway*'s gangway. As I tried to collect my senses I faltered and stumbled with the rise and fall of the boat's gunwales against the lower platform of the gangway. As the crew members tried to stabilise the buffeting craft with their outstretched boat-hooks, I felt almost compelled to cock a deaf 'un to some encouraging words of endearment which were streaming freely from the direction of the frantic coxswain who being in charge of the boat wanted nothing more than to get me safely inboard so that he could fold up for the night and get his head down.

After several attempts I was eventually assisted on to the ship's gangway, then having reached the top of the steps I tried to impress a very young officer of the watch by smartly cutting him a slice of cake. In other words I performed the age-old ritual of facing the quarterdeck and saluting. Such was my concentration that I tripped over my own feet and in a flash the duty quartermaster grabbed me under the arms in an attempt to lift me to an upright stance. Alas, I did not appreciate his helpful gesture. Due to my fogged-up brain I responded by charging towards him like an angry bull. Luckily for me the Regulating Chief Petty Officer Penfold arrived just in time to quell the situation before it really got out of hand. Taking me by the arm he said, 'Come on this isn't like you.' His easy-going manner commanded my instant respect and in seconds I had calmed down. Obviously satisfied that Penfold had taken command of the situation the officer was prudent enough to withdraw from the scene thus leaving me in the hands of the regulator. As soon as the officer of the watch was out of earshot, Penfold turned to me and said, 'For your own safety I have to put you in cells for the night.' He then added, 'I will take you down to get your hammock so that you can have a good night to sleep it off.'

The next morning I was awakened by the clanging of the cell door, to my surprise there stood Penfold with a cup of cocoa in one hand and a bucket in the other. 'Now, drink this and scrub out the cell then at 0900 I will take you before the officer of the watch and don't forget let me do the talking.' Then as he turned to leave he winked at me and said, 'Don't worry, everything will turn out right for you.'

I couldn't believe my luck when at 0905 I walked away from the quarterdeck with nothing more than a flea in my ear. For the remainder of the morning I sat in silence as these thoughts loomed up before me. Never again would I hear Penfold's triumphant cry, 'Got-yur,' when during his midnight rounds, he would frighten the life out of us gambling participants who would all be crouched over a pack of cards, but like Nelson he would turn a blind eye and say, 'Keep the noise down lads.' For those of us who lived on there remained only memories. We were the lucky ones who were given the privilege of knowing him.

By midday we survivors had been put ashore in Haifa. As soon as we landed on the quayside we were herded into lorries and taken to a disused army camp about half a mile out of town. Obviously the *Zulu*'s signalman had been busy on the way in because everything was so well organised, they even had a hot meal ready for us.

During dinner word was put around that we had all been allocated one of the huts on the opposite side of the compound to use as living quarters. Being anxious to get settled in I soon made my way towards the hut. As I entered the door, a corporal who was standing nearby pointed towards a pile of bedding in the corner and said, 'Grab yourself a mattress and a couple of blankets and bed yourself down on the floor.' Looking across the room I could hardly recognise the features of Stoker Gains. This old-timer who was well into his fifties was sitting on the bed with his back propped up against the wall after having been exposed to the most terrifying experience. Still in severe shock he sat staring into space while shaking from head to toe.

'All his skin looks scorched,' I remarked to one of his crew-mates.

'It's not surprising. He was watch below when it happened, it's a miracle how he got out of it,' came the reply.

The next morning, I ventured to have a chat with Gains. 'What happened to you Larry?' I asked.

In a trembling voice he answered me, 'I can't remember much, first there was a huge explosion the next thing I knew I was being fished out of the water.'

Still without footwear we were unable to venture far from the camp. Therefore we were somewhat relieved when one of the hands poked his head through the doorway shouting, 'Collect your shoes on the parade ground.' Within a couple of minutes the scene was like a strip from *Comic Cuts*. During the morning two vans had made a tour of all the shoe shops and stores in Haifa. It didn't take long for the lads to reason that the shoes would vary in size and quality. Within a few minutes all the shoes had been seized from their boxes and laid strewn all over the parade ground. There was so much disarray it became impossible to find a pair of matching shoes. Because we looked so bedraggled it was decided to call upon the army to kit us out. After paying a visit to the quartermaster's store I returned to my hut clutching two khaki shirts, two pairs of short trousers, two pairs of socks, two pairs of boots and a cap. By late afternoon we were all dressed up like tailor's dummies and ready to sample the beer in Haifa. However there was a snag none of us had any money. We were not about to be put off by such a trivial setback. Not a bit of it. Someone discovered that an enterprising Arab who was employed within the camp was offering a hundred piastres for each pair of boots. The news was spread around like wildfire. This was manna from heaven, it gave us new hope. Suddenly our fortunes had changed; we had all become solvent, but very short of footwear.

As the days passed the routine in the camp was gradually becoming more organised and after a week we heard that the paymaster was dishing out forty pounds per man to buy new kit. The snag was that there was no place in Haifa where a sailor could buy a uniform and once again I couldn't believe my luck. 'I have all this money to spend on beer,' I told myself. I think most of us had the same idea because within an hour the camp was like a ghost town.

Before I left the hut I walked across the room to have a few words with Stoker Gains who after all this time still had not received any medical treatment. There he was propped up against the wall and still shaking with shock.

Perhaps it's just as well that I could not remember much about the run ashore I had that night, to say the least it must have been hectic because I arrived back in the camp skint. During the morning I met up with Sam Hart again. He was beaming all over his chops, I had never seen him look so jubilant before.

'You look pleased with yourself,' I said.

'Shats, I have good news for you,' he burst out. 'We are joining the *Otus* this afternoon and sailing for home tomorrow.

Seized with panic, I gasped, 'Bloody hell I just blown all my kit money and I haven't a stitch to stand up in.' Sam must have read my thoughts.

Just as I was about to ask him for a loan, he said, 'I cannot help you Tom, I need what little I have to kit myself out.'

'Not to worry, there is bound to be someone on the *Otus* who will lend me a few quid,' I answered.

It was not by accident that our début with our new mess-mates coincided with the daily rum issue. I couldn't wish for a better opportunity to catch them in a generous mood. I thought it might be just the right setting to tap some unsuspecting soul for a rubber. When I arrived in the stokers' mess everything seemed to be going to plan. A group of half a dozen or so lads were sitting around the table eagerly awaiting their measure of rum.

As I sat down to join them a character by the name of Lenny Lamb looked up and said, 'Hello Shats what are you doing down here?'

'I have just come to join you to go home,' I answered. Then almost in the same breath, I asked, 'Who has all the money in the boat?' I studied his face while waiting for a reply. He was small in stature but a real Jack the lad type, he wore his hat perched on the back of his head and had two large front teeth protruding over his lower lip. This, together with a dancing glint in his eyes, blessed his whole countenance, suggesting a cheerful, easy-going and fun-loving individual. Such was my assessment, but I was soon to discover that these blessings served a dual purpose. They were the perfect camouflage to hide the practical joker beneath the surface.

In answer to my plea for money, Lamb replied, 'I am afraid that you are unlucky, you know what it is like we have spent all of ours on presents to take home.' Lamb listened to me explain my urgent need for cash, and he showed so much concern, it was clear he really wanted to help me. Suddenly he hit on an idea.

'Why don't you ask our engineer officer? He is loaded, the lads often go to him when they are short of cash.' He paused for a minute then added, 'He is coming back here in a minute with the chief stoker to check the stores and he will let you have it, he is a real toff, you'll see.'

'They are coming through now,' came a voice from the background.

As I looked towards the motor room, Lamb whispered, 'Now don't forget, all you have to say is – "How are you fixed for a rubber, Sam?"' Half-suspecting this unlikely source of finance, I searched the faces of my new crewmates for reassurance only to form the opinion that if Lamb was spinning me a line none of them was going to let the cat out of the bag.

Then quickly looking back to Lamb, 'Sam?' I queried.

'Yes that's right, he likes to be called by his first name, I told you he is one of the boys,' Lamb answered.

Before I had time to give further thought to the matter both the chief stoker and the engineer officer had entered the mess.

Clearing my throat I looked straight at the officer and boldly asked, 'How are you fixed for a rubber?' With my eyes transfixed on the officer's changing facial expression I nearly choked announcing his name, 'Sam.'

Suddenly there was such a scarper as all around me my mess-mates took to their heels like scalded cats while Sam stood before me with his eyes bulging out of their sockets and both cheekbones almost breaking through his lean cheeks. 'S— S— Sam,' he stuttered, 'Wh— Wh— Who are you calling Sam? Who are you? Get off my boat,' he screamed at me. Over his shoulder I could see the chief stoker doubled up and almost splitting his sides trying to stifle his laughter. In the meantime Sam was so outraged by this encounter that he had to pause to catch his breath. Immediately I took the opportunity to explain that I was the new stoker who had joined the boat to go home with it.

'That's what you think,' he yelled out. After a few seconds when Sam had regained his composure, he asked, 'Why do you need money?'

'I have to buy some kit because I lost all my gear on the *Medway*,' I answered.

'Were you with the others who got paid out forty pounds to buy new kit?' asked Sam.

'Yes but I spent it ashore last night,' I replied.

Once again Sam hit the roof. 'You spent forty pounds in

one night,' he yelled. Then without waiting for my reply he quickly turned tail and made tracks back towards the wardroom, and I felt quite sure that he had forgotten why he had come aft in the first place. Gradually my distant but captive audience returned to the mess, all except Lamb who remained on the casing above the after-hatch still rolled up with laughter.

Half in rage and yet still being able to see the funny side of it I yelled up to him. 'If you come down here you bastard I'll kill you.'

As the laughter subsided Lamb returned to the mess, 'I never thought that you would fall for that one, Shats. I thought you knew him, he doesn't drink he doesn't smoke and he never goes ashore. He is as tight as a duck's arse.'

Feeling completely shattered I wondered what would be the outcome of my request and being the complete optimist I shrugged my shoulders saying at least Sam hadn't flatly refused me.

Suddenly a voice in the motor room caused my stomach to turn over again. 'Will Stoker Shattock report to the engineer in the control room.'

'Your worries are over Shats, Sam is going to lend you the money,' shouted Lamb.

'You had better hope and pray that he hasn't got a draft chit for me to leave the boat,' I joked with him. 'I'll tell you one thing if I don't go home with this boat I will make bloody sure that you don't.'

When I reached the control room the engineer officer stood there waiting for me, then hardly looking at me he said, 'Follow me.' Without a word between us we walked together back to the camp which by this time was known as 'Medway 2'. Sam then led me into one of the smaller huts which had a temporary notice pinned to the door. The office was occupied by a bearded paymaster and two writers. Addressing the former Sam asked, 'Can this man have a casual payment?' and once again I became the focus of attention as I tried to explain how I blew forty pounds in one run ashore. After I supplied the paymaster with my name and official number he appointed one of the writer's to open the ledger and find the corresponding details.

'How much do you require?' he asked.

'Can I have forty pounds?' I asked in a somewhat timid voice.

The paymaster looked at Sam as if to reassure himself that his hearing was okay. By now it became evident that Sam was more uneasy than I was. He threw both arms in the air in a gesture of despair and ran out of the office shouting, 'Let him have as much as he wants,' leaving me to face the embarrassment of collecting it.

A quarter of an hour later I bounced back into the stokers' mess tossing my cap full of piastre notes high in the air leaving them to rain down like falling confetti. While my mess-mates looked sick with envy I boasted, 'Now it's my turn to laugh, I am the only one here with money and I am keeping every cent of it.'

'You are not going ashore again?' queried Lamb.

'Just you bloody watch me,' I answered. I scooped the notes off the table and crammed them into my pocket and made straight for the gangplank.

Later that night I returned to the boat with very little to show out of the forty piastre notes which I had such a hard time obtaining. In fact the only clothing that I bought was a set of dungarees. From my own observations as I clambered my way past the crew-space I became aware that the duty-watch had been extremely busy while I had been ashore.

The decks in the fore-ends and the crew space were packed so high with cases, that even I of moderate height, had to stoop when passing through the boat. All this weight I thought, if we dive like this we will never get up again, then to add to my fears I shuddered when I saw 'No smoking' signs that hung at frequent intervals throughout the boat.

'Is it ammo?' I asked one of the seaman.

'That's not the half of it, number three battery tank is full of it,' came the reply. Then to pile on the agony he went on to say that some of the external tanks were full of high octane aviation spirit and that the boat had shed its drop-keel. It had also left number three battery in Alexandria. It was now quite evident that my trip home was not going to be the cushy cruise through the Med which I had hoped for.

During that stage of the war the allied armies had been driven back almost into Alexandria. With the absence of fighters and anti-aircraft ammunition Malta had no means to defend herself and was then under siege. In a desperate bid to supply the island with these necessities, operation code name 'Pedestal' was launched. It was the largest convoy ever to set sail for Malta. Our losses were enormous. The loss of nine merchant ships, one aircraft carrier, two cruisers and one destroyer together with a badly damaged aircraft carrier and two cruisers was a bitter pill to swallow. The remaining five merchant ships were also badly damaged but they did manage to limp into Malta's Grand Harbour. The most vital of these was the large tanker *Ohio* which with two destroyers strapped to her sides did manage to deliver the bulk of her cargo unharmed.

Although our loses were heavy the enemy did not come away unscathed. Our submarines torpedoed two of their cruisers and one of their submarines. Expensive? Well that may be, but without the vital supplies ferried by those ships, Malta would not have survived. A few of our larger submarines also did a big delivery job when no other ships could get through. From time to time the so-called magic carpet was put into operation when they would run the gauntlet between Alexandria and Malta. Back in Haifa we on the *Otus* were about to embark on such a mission. I knew the trip home would not be easy but never in my wildest dreams had I bargained for the epic which time alone would unfold.

Soon after putting to sea we were called to diving stations in order to exercise our trim. At the sound of the klaxon all main vent levers were pulled open and the hydroplanes set hard to dive, then as both screws thrashed away at the sea I waited for the sensation of being plunged into the depths. Can you imagine my surprise when the needle on the depth gauge remained at zero feet?

Years afterwards I was reminded of the incident when reading a letter written by Lieutenant R. Lister who was our Jimmy at the time. It read, 'I was faced with the problem of having to stow away large quantities of food, spares, ammo, and petrol, all destined for delivery in Malta. I remember that when we tried to trim after leaving Haifa I had one hell of a job in getting the bugger to go under, having miscalculated the weight on board and having to shed our ten-ton keel to compensate for the extra weight the task was not an easy one.' After half an hour or so the frustrated first lieutenant and a much flustered pump room operator between them managed to stabilise the boat to some measure of respectability. Perhaps understandably such a scene in the control room would often arouse grins of mirth and silent sniggers on the faces of bystanding watch-keepers. It would all seem great fun to those who were not implicated. I think it also helped to cover up the nervous tension of all concerned. Eventually to everyone's relief we were once again on the surface with both engines racing ahead with our bows pointing towards the west.

After a few hours things began to go wrong in the engine room. It was towards the end of the morning watch when we in the engine room had reason to concern ourselves about the development of an unfamiliar clattering noise apparently coming from the rear end of the starboard engine. The noise became so loud that it almost drowned the din created by other components of the clapped out diesels. Within seconds of being called, our warrant engineer, Sam Hocking, together with Charlie Negus, our chief ERA, hurried to inspect the offending part of the engine and after a short discussion decided to keep it running until we dived at first light.

As far as I was concerned it meant that all my thoughts of shut-eye would be out of the question for at least another eight hours. As soon as the boat was submerged the engine room stokers were detailed to assist the ERAs to correct the annoying setback. It was obvious that the fault had occurred inside the clutch housing. To gain access to the damaged parts we first had to dismantle the surrounding gantry as well as the clutch housing. After removing these and many other obstructions we finally came to grips with the cause of the trouble, the bolt heads which secured the clutch coupling to the flywheel had been sheared off. Due to the distorted hull the engine mountings had moved, thus causing the misalignment of the starboard engine main shaft. To rectify this completely would require nothing less than a major refit which of course couldn't be carried out at sea. Therefore the only option open to the engineer would be that of a patching up job and for this he was fully prepared. Before leaving Alexandria he had shipped aboard a large steel trunk which was filled to the top with replacement nuts and bolts.

At daybreak every morning as soon as the boat dived, the engine room team would set about the same task of clearing the obstructions so that the ERAs could replace the bolts that had sheared off during the previous night. Working in temperatures which soared above one hundred and twenty degrees and being up to our necks in oil and grease, this was not my idea of fun. By the time we had reached Malta five days later we could have done the job blindfolded.

It was early the next morning when the *Otus* came to rest alongside the oiling wharf in Malta harbour and as soon as the hatches were opened the task of unloading the precious stores and ammo became the immediate priority. While the stokers hurried to connect the hoses ready to discharge the petroleum the seamen worked like beavers removing number three battery covers in order to gain access to the ammo which was so urgently needed by the gun crews engaged in the island's defence. Forming a human chain case after case was passed out of the boat and on to waiting trucks on the quay.

The surrounding devastation caused by recent air raids was sufficient incentive for all to get stuck into it and get the job done so that we could get to hell out of it as soon as possible. Keeping a watchful eye on the skies above I felt intensely impatient as I waited for the completion of the operation. We knew that we were sitting ducks and thoughts of what could have happened had we been caught in the midst of discharging our volatile cargo had to be cast aside. Thankfully Lady Luck was on our side that day and we managed to complete the task before the raiders returned.

By that time our captain, Lieutenant Clutterbuck had decided that he would no longer present our boat as an easy target for the returning marauders to blow to smithereens. He moved us out to deeper waters where we battened down the hatches and dived to the bottom. Once there we could continue our repairs to the engines without interruption. While we stokers enjoyed the luxury of working in two watches our chief ERA, Charlie Negus, laboured at the sharp end for almost two days without leaving the engine room.

During the second day I was just about to start my stint, when my attention was drawn to a small group of my mess-mates who were sitting in the motor room. They had become engrossed in the study of the Chief Tiffy's fundamental anatomy – the chief's only attire hung round his waist in the form of a sarong and it was very skimpy to say the least. At the time he was busy replacing one of the exhaust boxes. Because it was so awkward to get to, Charlie had to sit in a squat position with feet astride, balancing on top of the crank shaft casing. He had therefore unwittingly become the object of ridicule by exposing his assets to all and sundry. With his undercarriage dangling perilously close to the bottom of the oily crankcase sump, he sure looked a funny spectacle. What was most amusing, was the expression on the engineer officer's face when from a vantage point just behind the chief he got the full display almost under his nose. All this was funny enough but when the officer looked up towards the motor room and saw the gloating audience which he had been entertaining, the coy look on his face caused an outburst of hysterical laughter.

At the end of the third day none of us was sorry to leave Malta. I did have one run ashore but the only refreshment available was the local wine, which I have never ventured to taste since; the stuff nearly blew my head off. With Malta behind us I can remember thinking that we had now completed the most dangerous part of our voyage home and up to now we had been lucky enough to come through unscathed. All that was needed was for our luck to hold while probing our way through the dreaded minefields of the Pantelleria Straits. Still imprinted on my mind were thoughts of my first encounter with that curtain of terror which had become the ultimate challenge to test the skill of a submarine's asdic operator, 'Ping Bosun'. It happened a little over two years previously when we narrowly escaped disaster on the *Tetrarch*. That was when we first came out to the Mediterranean, but sadly she was not so lucky on her return trip home. She was lost somewhere between Malta and Gibraltar and I would take an educated guess that the Pantelleria Straits was her graveyard. The area around the minefield was known to be regularly patrolled by enemy 'E' boats so our captain was prudent enough to submerge the boat long before we reached the narrows.

Late that night the captain aided by the skill of the asdic operator began to ease the boat through the minefield. As we in the engine room sat around in small groups, a sudden chill ran down my spine when what sounded like a wire hawser scraped along the full length of the boat, then for a breathtaking moment I sat looking up at the hull above me. I had hardly time to draw my breath when another sound of screeching metal froze every nerve in my body until once again it had travelled the full length of the hull. As I waited and listened for the boat to get clear I could have heard a pin drop and it seemed that several minutes had passed before any of us spoke.

'I think we are clear,' someone whispered. Then as time passed our pent up fears gave way to boisterous laughter as nervous tension gradually subsided. Soon our captain decided that it was safe enough to blow main ballast and continue towards Gibraltar on the surface.

Although daily repairs to the engine clutch were becoming painfully monotonous, we almost arrived at Gibraltar without suffering further hazards. I say almost for this reason – while entering harbour our captain tried to sink Gibraltar by ramming it. We were cruising towards the mole when the captain suddenly realised that the boat was travelling too fast and that he had left it too late to turn. The only thing that he could do then was to go full astern both. Not realising that such a manoeuvre could not be carried out without first disengaging the engine clutches he rang the engine room telegraphs full astern. This impossible order caused confusion between the engine room and the motor room watchkeepers and valuable seconds were lost. By the time the engine clutches were out and the main motors ready 'grouped up' to go 'full astern', we were almost knocked off our feet and we heard one almighty crunch as the *Otus* ploughed into the mole. Luckily the boat only suffered superficial damage and we were able to continue homeward bound a few days later.

In the midst of the humdrum life in a submarine in wartime a few enthusiastic animal lovers still found time to look after pets. It so happened that while we were in Gibraltar my attention was drawn to one of the crew of the *P222* as he paced up and down the quay followed by three ducks, each of which was harnessed to a lead. It was amusing to watch the fostered three wobbling on behind spontaneously expressing their approval with loud quack, quacks. The scene before me would have been worthy to have aroused the inspiring mind of Disney. Was this caring foster parent half duck or were the ducks half human? It would have been my guess that with a few strokes of his pen the brilliant cartoonist would have dressed the ducks in the rig of the day complete with the submarine cap-band and all. I suppose any normal thinking person would regard three live ducks as an unlikely addition to the crew's cramped quarters in the fore-ends, but having previously witnessed a slightly inebriated mess-mate trying to lead a donkey across a submarine's narrow gangplank, any other species from the animal kingdom would be quite acceptable as far as I was concerned.

Two days later I joined forces with a few of my mess-mates who were being entertained by the antics of a couple of the *P222*'s crew. Seemingly they were having a whale of a time trying to grab hold of the ducks as they flew about inside the steel structure beneath the bridge. The snag was that an hour earlier the two seamen had just completed a splendid red oxide painting job on the rusty iron work. Whoever it was who let the ducks into such an environment could have been anyone's guess. As the two volunteers who went to their rescue climbed and slid all over the iron girders they were yelling out curses which would have reddened the cheeks of hardened sailors. After ten minutes or so the two finally emerged looking like Red Indians clutching large bundles of red feathers which once were ducks.

'How the bloody hell are we to clean them up?' one of them shouted.

In double quick time the problem was solved. There is nothing that can't be cleaned with a bucket of shale oil and a bar of purser's hard soap. They would be as good as new in half an hour, or at least that is what they thought. All was well until some bright spark put them over the side to rinse them out, unhappily the poor creatures had lost all of their natural oils from their plumage, causing them to sink to the bottom like lead weights. When Davy Jones found them on his dinner table he must have thought that Christmas had come early. Sadly when Christmas did arrive, there were to be no celebrations for the families of the crew of *P222*. On her very next patrol she was lost with all hands. Was there an omen somewhere?

Nautical hopscotch; that is my interpretation of our boat's performance during the remaining part of our voyage home. It was stop, mend, dive, surface, almost every inch of the way. The barometer fell as we approached the English Channel and the raging seas tossed and pummelled our steel hulk as though it was a floating cork. With each wave our stern would rise out of the water only to come crashing down again. The shocking punishment to the screws and shaft wreaked havoc with our already damaged engine clutch. While wondering whether or not the boat would stay together long enough to reach our nearest port, which was Plymouth, we received a signal ordering us to proceed up the Irish Sea and round the top of Scotland. From my worm's eye view I could not grasp the logic behind the orders. To travel all that way to get to the Tyne, Don't they want us to get home I asked myself?

As the *Otus* continued to battle its way through the storm the terrific battering of the mountainous waves had taken its toll on the exhaust muffler tank, and as the result dense black smoke trailed behind us. By nightfall our presence became even more conspicuous as showers of red sparks illuminated the boat giving a spectacular firework display. As we approached Cape Wrath the conditions on the bridge became so dangerous that the captain decided that it would be wiser to rest up in a loch inside one of the remote islands rather than flirt with an impending tragedy.

The next morning as we continued eastwards through the Pentland Firth, a westerly gale combined with a strong easterly tide, stirred up an enormous following sea. It was years after when Lieutenant Lister wrote:

> I was scared bloody stiff, we were pooped every few minutes by green seas swamping the bridge. To prevent being swept away we had to lash ourselves to the periscope standard. Our ordeal was made worse by having to stop engines and shut the conning tower hatch each time the raging sea engulfed the bridge.

Throughout the day the seamen continued to battle against the odds with vigour determination and courage, but as dusk fell once again they had to submit to the hostile elements. With the protecting haven of Scapa-Flow off our port bow the temptation was too great for our captain to resist. The following morning when we turned south into the North Sea, there was a vast improvement in the weather. The storm had abated and for the first time in days I had every expectation of reaching our destination, Blyth. I think everyone in the boat let out a great sigh of relief when the *Otus* finally tied up alongside the quay the following morning.

The run up the Tyne to Swan Hunters' yard became the final test of endurance for our clapped out engines. Before leaving Blyth we took on board a dozen or so civil engineers who crowded the engine room taking all sorts of readings while we on watch set the engines to their maximum speed. At times I thought the whole lot was going to blow up as the din was deafening. When the telegraph rang down from the bridge 'stop main engines', 'out engine clutch' the two donkeys were on their last knockings, they could not have made another stroke.

Chapter Nine

And Mother Came Too

After getting married during my Christmas leave, I returned to Wallsend with my wife. There I remained with the s/m *Otus* until March when to my surprise I was recalled to the submarine base HMS *Dolphin*. Although I was living the life of Riley on 'lodge and comp' I was not sorry to leave because only a few days before Warrant Officer Hocking refused my promotion to acting leading stoker. To my mind there was no justification for him to have done so and if that is what he thought of me, I would be better off away from it all I thought. Very soon my wife and I were happily boarding a southbound train from Newcastle. When I arrived at the Dolphin I stood in the middle of Platypus hut, trying to come to terms with my surroundings. During my three years' absence nothing had been done to improve the comfort of its occupants; with its bare tables, long bench seats and dim lighting the whole scene looked as austere as it did on the first day that I had set eyes on it.

After being detailed for work the next morning I was soon to discover that my status as a seasoned submariner, gave me no right to the privileged occupations enjoyed by the chosen few. Instead I was given a menial job of sweeping the non-existent dirt off the spotless floors of the machine shop. Why I had to make myself look busy doing nothing for eight hours a day was beyond my comprehension. It seemed to me that such practices took place in most shore establishments. I think it was a ploy to discourage genuine seafarers from getting too settled in, or what otherwise was known as becoming barrack stanchions.

After a month of boredom I was happy to be drafted to the s/m *Sirdar*. She was one of the new 'S' class submarines which was little more than a hull tied up in the basin in Vickers' Yard in Barrow in Furness. The news delighted me because a draft chit to Barrow in those days was one of the most sought-after moves by all submariners. I knew that I would be living ashore on lodge and comp for which I would receive a weekly allowance which was deemed to be generous by the standards of that time. Being newly married the extra money would enable my wife and I to set up a temporary home for as long as my stay would last. We could also buy a few extra luxuries that we could not otherwise afford.

After a twenty-four hour journey I arrived at my destination completely shagged and in no mood to hunt for digs. This being so I welcomed the news that my guide had already arranged for me to share his excellent lodgings with four other ratings who had been standing by the s/m *Vandal*. After a five minute cab drive I was greeted by a middle-aged woman who dwelled in a terraced house where I was to stay until such time the s/m *Sirdar* was ready for trails. For a brief spell I remained in those comfortable quarters and I felt quite at ease with my friendly compatriots. As for our landlady she was a diamond, no chore was too much for her to handle and I would have been more than happy to have stayed there, but this was not to be. Owing to a shortage of accommodation I was obliged to move into the house next door when after spending a weekend at my home in Kent I brought my wife back to Barrow.

After introducing my wife to Mrs Hall my new landlady,

it was decided that from then on my wife would be cooking all my meals. We were told that we could have the use of the gas stove in the kitchen and all the cooking utensils. The next morning I left my wife to do the shopping while I was kept busy in the boat learning the whereabouts of all the controls to operate the various machines that had been fitted in the boat by Vickers' engineers.

Later that day when I arrived back in my digs my wife showed some concern about the breakfast meals that Mrs Hall had been cooking for me prior to my wife's arrival in Barrow. She explained that she had spent the whole morning cleaning out the oven and the cooking utensils because everywhere she looked she found mice droppings. I almost threw up on the front-room carpet when she told me that Mrs Hall had been cooking my breakfast in a mixture of solidified fat and mice droppings which she kept in a frying pan in the bottom of the oven.

'Didn't you notice anything?' asked my wife.

'Well I was a bit puzzled because every morning before eating my bacon and egg I would push what I thought to be well baked breadcrumbs to one side of the plate. The old lady must be as blind as a bat,' I said.

As the days slipped by I was hardly aware that the *Vandal* had already been turned over to the Admiralty and was starting its trials. Soon after it left Barrow, Mrs Rayburn my former land lady came to the door sobbing her heart out. She had got word that the *Vandal* had been lost on its trials.

'My poor dear boys, they have all been lost, they were so young,' she was saying between sobs.

As regards my own feelings it was a very sad loss. It was bad enough to lose one of ours to the enemy but to lose one on its trials, surely someone had blundered. It took quite a while for us to get over the shock. But that wasn't all because a month later, another new submarine suffered the same fate on its trials. Yet again we had to forget and get on with the job.

After those Mediterranean patrols, life in Barrow had become Utopia itself. Having little else to do I found myself employed as the engineer officer's runabout and general dogsbody. This soft number gave me plenty of time to live it up ashore, the only snag was that I did not always have enough money to keep up with the lifestyle of my shore-side compatriots. I was always on the lookout to make a bob or two. One morning the *Sirdar*'s engineer officer asked me to clean out one of the offices.

'Get rid of the rubbish and leave it nice and tidy,' he said. He told me that it had been occupied by another engineer officer whose boat had left Barrow to start its trials early that morning. While dusting the shelves I couldn't believe my luck when my eyes focused on a pair of neatly folded trousers inside one of the cubby holes. Being fully convinced that the officer had left Barrow for good I could hardly be blamed for thinking that he no longer wanted them. While rubbing my hands together and thinking that they would fetch a few bob, I held them up against myself as thoughts of an instant buyer flashed through my mind. They would just about fit my landlord, I thought. As soon as my boss gave me the okay to go to lunch, I packed my neatly wrapped parcel under my arm and went racing towards my digs on the other side of the town.

When I arrived at the house my landlady was standing inside the doorway.

'Is Mr Hall about?' I enquired.

'Yes, go through, he is in the living room,' she answered.

Then poking my head round the door I shouted, 'Do you want to buy a pair of trousers cheap?' Looking up from his comfortable armchair it seemed to take him a few seconds before he could grasp the significance of my unexpected question.

Then handing him the trousers I said, 'Just take a look at

them, give me thirty bob and they are yours.'

Just then his wife came in, 'They do look smart go and try them on,' she urged.

After popping upstairs for a couple of minutes the delighted Mr Hall returned to the room beaming all over his face. 'They fit like a glove,' he said.

'Yes,' agreed his wife, 'you look a real bobby dazzler in them.'

She then went to her purse and handed me the money. Spurred on by my newly found wealth I could not resist a call at the local before returning to the office. When I eventually did arrive back, it was as though all hell had been let loose.

The engineer officer came charging towards me, 'Where on earth have you been?' he was shouting. 'I have got people searching all over the place looking for you.' Not waiting to hear my answer, he then fired the fifty dollar question, 'Did you find a pair of trousers this morning?'

I stood there in silence while searching my imagination for an excuse to offer him.

'Well, answer me,' he snapped. 'Did you or did you not find the trousers?'

'Yes,' I answered.

'Well where are they?' he asked.

'I have sold them,' I faltered.

'You had better go and buy them back again, because the engineer officer has an appointment with the admiral of the dockyard and he is furious because he is already an hour late.'

'I cannot buy them back, sir, because I have spent nearly all of the money,' I explained.

To my surprise he didn't blow his top.

'How much do you need?'

'I think a pound will be enough, sir,' I answered.

After fishing about in different pockets it seemed quite

evident that he was as skint as I was. Eventually he did manage to come up with the goods and I was soon on my way to collect the trousers. As I raced towards my digs I thanked my lucky stars that I had not flogged them to some stranger in one of the pubs, had I done so I could have definitely waved goodbye to them. My only worry now was, how Mr Hall would take it when I asked for them back. As luck would have it he was quite good about it and when I told them about the panic it had caused, both he and his wife fell about all over the place laughing but this was no time for me to join in the merriment. It was a sweltering hot afternoon and I still had a two mile run before I could hand over the trousers to the rightful owner.

Half an hour later I arrived at the boat out of breath, a stitch in my side and soaking wet with sweat. Much to my relief the trot sentry was the only person in sight. As he stood on the casing grinning from ear to ear, I breathlessly asked where the engineer officer was.

'He is walking about the boat half-dressed and boy oh boy does he want to see you. He is doing his nut,' he answered.

Having no wish to come face to face with a distraught officer dressed in a cheese cutter and tunic, I pushed the trousers into the arms of the bewildered sentry. 'Here you take them to him,' I said. I then took to my heels and ran like the clappers until the boat was out of sight.

Soon after, the *Sirdar*'s engineer told me that he had some good news for me. In a somewhat puzzled tone of voice, he said, 'You will be pleased to know that your advancement to acting leading stoker has just been sent to me from the Admiralty. In the meantime I will send for a replacement for you and when he arrives you will be transferred to s/m *Vampire*.'

Soon after I made arrangements to bring my wife up from Kent. At the time she was five months' pregnant, but life expectancy being short we were determined to make the most of every minute of our time together. She remained with me until two weeks before the baby was due, I then had to take her back home for her confinement. The day before I was due back in Barrow she was rushed to hospital in agonising pain which resulted in a life-threatening haemorrhage. The trouble was most likely caused when she had a nasty fall while stepping into an old tin bath a couple of weeks earlier while we were in digs. For a while it was touch and go for both mother and unborn baby. With the help of the doctor I managed to get extended leave so I was able to be near her when she gave birth to a healthy bouncing baby boy. As soon as she was out of danger I had to return to Barrow leaving my wife and son at home in Kent, but the separation did not last for long. When my wife was up and about again she wrote and asked me to come and fetch them, so that we could all spend the last week together before starting trials on the *Vampire*.

When I wrote explaining that I could not get leave, she decided to come on her own, but my mother wouldn't hear of it. She said that the journey was much too far for a young mother and baby to travel on their own so she decided to come with them. I felt a bit of a nit when I told my messmates that my mother had come to see us off, but my embarrassment was soon forgotten when on their first visit to the boat they received a friendly welcome.

After the first introductions I was astonished by the apparent easy manner in which my mother was accepted.

'This calls for a celebration,' agreed my two pals, Nick and Blonde. 'Tonight we must all go out and wet the baby's head.'

'Who do think is going to look after the baby?' I asked.

'Don't worry,' replied Blonde, 'I know a couple of girls whose mother will look after the baby. I can also borrow a pram,' he said.

As far as my wife was concerned this momentous occasion became the ideal excuse to gratify her latest whim. She wanted me to buy a new hat that she had seen in a shop window earlier that day. During those austere times it was quite unusual to find such a large display of artistic creations so readily available for purchase, so perhaps my wife could be forgiven for her self-indulgence regarding the price tag. By late that afternoon she was the proud owner of what could be described as a small pillbox-shaped black velvet hat which was adorned by a fine black lace veil. This unique masterpiece was one of six models each of which was supposedly worn by different film stars. This particular one was known as the Hedy Lamarr look.

It was seven o'clock in the evening when Blonde, Jim, and their two girls arrived at my digs with the pram. Then what a commotion, everybody seemed so high-spirited. I felt as though I was going to a carnival. There we were all togged up to the nines and it seemed as if the whole street had turned out to see us off. Mrs Hall came wobbling to the front door holding out an umbrella, 'Here you had better take this with you, it looks as if it is going to rain.'

This fat jolly lady had never spoken a truer word in her life. The rain couldn't have caught us in a worse spot there wasn't any shelter in sight, it didn't just pour it bucketed down. While the four women struggled to keep dry under the umbrella, I went tearing through the streets with the pram like Stirling Moss. With Blonde and Jim on my heels laughing like hyenas I was unaware of the fainter cries of help coming from the disgruntled women who were miles behind us slipping and sliding all over the wet cobbled stones in their high-heeled shoes. When we arrived at the girls' house, my wife, mother, baby and one of the girls went inside while the rest of us went racing towards the pub which was on the corner of the street about a hundred yards away. With the steam rising off our clothes we soon settled in for a boozy night. We were well into the second drink when I looked across the crowded lounge just in time to see my wife trying to make an unobtrusive entrance into the warm bar.

Sadly her efforts were shattered when I stood in the middle of the room and announced, 'Look everybody here comes Hedy Lamarr.' For some reason this unwanted attention seemed to annoy my wife; admittedly she did look a little bedraggled as she stood in the entrance with black mascara running down her cheeks and soaking wet hair hanging down like rats' tails, and as for the hat it now looked no more glamorous than a char's floppy mop stuck on her head. After spending some time in the ladies her tantrums gradually gave way to smiles when she returned to the party to join in the fun.

All too soon the evening sped by and it was a long time after last orders before our congenial host began to show obvious signs of losing his patience while accompanying us to the door. Then just for a few seconds the open door illuminated the dark wet street exaggerating the intensity of the glistening rain. We stood in the doorway just long enough to hear the bolts slam shut behind us, then suddenly the quite empty street became awakened by the hollow sound of clattering heels as we ran up hill towards the baby minder's house. When the good lady answered the door with a shush, we were not surprised when she whispered that the baby had been as good as gold and that he had slept all through the evening. The little blighter was like that, he would only wake up when everybody else wanted to go to sleep. After thanking the lady for looking after the baby, a couple of us gently lifted the pram and the sleeping baby over the front door steps and on to the pavement.

While my wife was seeing to the hood and checking that the baby was nice and snug she suddenly turned to me and snapped, 'Well put the umbrella up, I am getting soaked to the skin.' Not wishing to be relegated to the doghouse again I immediately complied with her wishes. I let go of the pram's handlebar and in one movement, opened up the umbrella raising it high into the air.

As I did so my frantic wife started to scream, 'My hat, my hat!'

'Where in hell is it?' I asked.

'It's caught up in the umbrella you silly twit,' she mocked.

I lowered the umbrella to see what had happened and there it was perched on the top like a bloody seagull. During the commotion we both let go of the pram and the next thing that I knew it was racing down the hill with my wife running after it screaming out, 'The baby, the baby!' Luckily she was able to catch up with the pram before it did any damage.

Eventually our good times in Barrow drew to a close. Most of the civil engineers had left the boat leaving just a couple behind to cope with the last minute adjustments. Weeks before I had chosen what then looked like the ideal billet to sling my hammock, then at the very last minute one of the fitters welded an open-topped electric boiler to the bulkhead right beside it. Needless to say my thoughts of what was bound to happen when we put to sea left me standing in the middle of the fore-ends cursing and swearing until the air was blue. I had not long to wait before I got my first drenching. It happened during our first night in the Irish Sea, when some silly bugger filled the tank to the brim. I had climbed into my hammock and was just dozing off when a sudden lurch to port removed the lid from the top of the tank swamping my middle parts with a deluge of scalding hot water. This caused me the most severe pain in the most tender parts of my anatomy. As I let go with one almighty yell I leapt from my hammock and went hopping up and down the fore-ends clutching my middle showing all the facial ferocity of a tribal war dancer.

After that I tried sleeping with an oilskin coat draped across the hammock. That was all right until we took on full stores. Then I found that the coxswain had stacked sacks of potatoes and cabbages on which rested the bottom of my hammock and when after a few days at sea they began to stink to high heaven that was too much for me to suffer so in the end I had to give in and find a another billet. I settled for a small place behind the port engine.

As the engines roared away hour after hour the chief ERA told me that he was amazed how I could sleep so well with all the noise.

'It's great, all that cool fresh air blowing down on me from that fan up there, it's lovely and comfortable,' I assured him. At least a month had passed before I found out that the fresh air was the discharge from the main battery cooling system therefore it contained poisonous gas fumes which probably would account for me sleeping so well.

After losing the s/ms *Vandal* and *Untamed* during their trials only a few months earlier, it was a great relief when all tests aboard the *Vampire* were exercised successfully. All that remained was to prepare the crew for wartime operations, hence the Shakedown patrol, which was designed to familiarise the crew with all aspects of their duties.

The atrocious weather that befell us during the following two weeks above all else demanded expert seamanship and dedicated skill to overcome the most appalling gales that I had ever witnessed. So violent was the storm that during one of my watches in the engine room the camshaft oil dipsticks which were normally housed about thirty degrees off the vertical, went flying across the engine room with all the force of a rocket-powered missile as each gigantic wave pounded the hull of the small submarine.

Why the boat didn't turn upside down was nothing less than a miracle. As for making contact with enemy shipping nothing was achieved regards shortening the war but one thing was for sure, that patrol was right for the inexperienced young sailors to cut their teeth on.

Having completed her first patrol, the *Vampire* pulled alongside one of the parent ships. Then as I stepped from the fore hatch on to the casing, my senses were alerted to rousing cheers coming from the direction of a boisterous welcoming party on the fore-well deck.

'That's him, Stoker Shattock,' I heard some one shout out.

Then another voice that I recognised immediately. It was that of Ginger Hepworth, 'Who flogged the officer's trousers?' he taunted.

By this time I had reached the top of the gangway, 'How do you know about that?' I asked.

'The whole fleet knows about it. When the admiral was being kept waiting for the engineer to turn up, he sent a signal which was promptly answered by another signal giving the full explanation as to why the engineer couldn't get there on time.

'Bloody hell, nothing like this has happened since the battle of Trafalgar,' I said.

I had become as famous as Nelson. I could just imagine the signal. 'With or without trousers, England expects!'

Chapter Ten

Misplaced Loyalties

Sadly this narration has reached a point which opposes all that I have implied regards the comradeship among submarine crews. Although I have had reservations of the need to disclose the ugly side of what can happen to men of different temperaments and backgrounds, I feel compelled to do so. The discomfort of living in a confined space during long spells at sea soon becomes a recipe for bad tempers. To win through such adversities requires resolute determination of well-trained men, equipped with a good sense of humour. I was soon to discover that such attributes were in short supply as far as my new crew-mates were concerned. As regards the stokers, almost without exception none of these men had been at sea before, so perhaps the forthcoming events would not seem too surprising. Although I feel the need to record these happenings, I have no wish to stigmatise the personnel involved. It is my opinion that any shortcomings hereby portrayed in their behaviour was the direct result of hurried training. For this reason neither the boat or its occupants shall be named.

Having completed the leading stoker's course, I returned to Dolphin and after two weeks I was once again drafted north to stand by a new submarine whilst it was being built. At least that is what I thought. When I arrived at the quay I was somewhat disappointed when I discovered that my holidays were over. The boat was fully commissioned with its full crew of officers and ratings and was already to start its working up trials. Feeling very scruffy after an all-night train journey, I laboured with my kitbag and hammock across the narrow gangplank. As I stepped on to the casing I saw the engineer officer awaiting my arrival.

As I approached him his face lit up with a smile as he greeted me with the words, 'You must be Leading Stoker Shattock, I have been expecting you.'

Somewhat surprised by this extraordinary meeting I stood there with mixed feelings of embarrassment and pleasure. 'I am told that you were on the *Thrasher*,' he added.

'That's correct. I was,' I answered.

Obviously feeling very pleased, his face beamed with delight as he welcomed me aboard. After the engineer's departure I couldn't help wondering what sort of a prize he thought he had won and I became a little worried about his expectations of me. After all, my knowledge of submarines did not extend beyond the bounds expected of a humble stoker. Little did I realise that a few days at sea would dispel all my expectations of future happiness among my fellow crew-mates. It was during one of our early dives when sudden cries of panic could be heard in the after-ends. The stoker on watch was shouting out, 'Water is pouring into the compartment.'

At the time I was lying on my bunk which was adjacent to the after-ends and for a few seconds I watched as three men became drenched in blinding spray while they made desperate attempts to find the source of the influx of water. As I looked one glance was enough to remind me of my very first patrol on the *Tetrarch*. The scene before me was the exact replica of what had happened then. After a few seconds I shot out of my bunk and raced towards the compressors, then shutting my eyes I reached through the spray to find the water-cooling shut-off valves and with a few turns I shut them off. Having stopped the gush of water I was about to return to my bunk when the engineer officer appeared on the scene and began to question the outside leading stoker about leaving the valves open. The air compressors had been used the night before so it seemed quite obvious that the person who operated them failed to shut down afterwards.

After strenuously denying his negligence the leading stoker turned to me and shouted, 'You must have opened them because you went straight to them.'

In answer to his accusation I replied that I had seen it happen before and in any case I had no reason to go near the after-ends because none of the machinery there was within my sphere of duty. This whole experience left me speechless. There was I expecting to be commended for my alert efficiency but instead I was to become the scapegoat for someone who was not man enough to admit his mistake. The vacuum created by the engineer's departure from the mess became immediately replaced by an atmosphere of mistrust and suspicion. I felt like an innocent party who had been placed in a compromising situation by an unknown thief. Feeling deeply wounded I had yet to endure the final thrust. It happened about an hour later when the engineer returned to the mess and began to address half a dozen of us who were sitting at the table. In a condescending tone he suggested that one of us may have been practising opening and shutting the valves. He then added that while he regarded such practices to be commendable, that we must for heaven's sake remember to shut them afterwards.

Because of his constant gaze in my direction I thought his insinuations were most unfair and as far as he was concerned I was the guilty party and nothing was going to change his mind about it. The idea that I was the culprit was absolutely ludicrous. As a trained submariner I was appalled by his complete disregard of my record and previous experience. Up to that time I had completed thirty patrols during most of which I operated the identical machinery in the after-ends. I wouldn't have cared so much if the outside leading stoker had been present when the Engineer came up with this crazy idea, but his absences assured me that as far as the engineer was concerned he was completely exonerated from all blame. In a way I was not surprised that the engineer did believe him, because he was quite capable of charming the birds from the trees.

During the next month or so the climate in the mess, although by no means perfect, was for the most part tolerable. As on most ships there was always the odd youngster who would shirk his part of the mess chores. On such occasions it was my job to bring them into line by ordering them to get on with the particular task in question. This would often cause resentment among the culprits and it wasn't long before a few of them began to gang up and buck against my authority. Such challenges became much more frequent after the engineer's ridiculous hypothesis concerning the burst safety disc on the after-end air compressors. It became obvious to me that I was not imagining things when I thought that the engineer had pointed the accusing finger in my direction. From then on it seemed to me that I had become an open target for ridicule.

Although the snide remarks and mutterings which I was often subjected to would sometimes make me very angry, it would not be fair of me to put all the blame on the offenders. It could not have been easy for young men to be suddenly uprooted from the security of their home environment to find themselves in the midst of wartime operations in a confined submarine but nevertheless it was surprising how many could cope with the situation. At that stage of the war it was nothing exceptionable for the boat to be manned by so many inexperienced stokers. However this time there was one very important difference from the other boats which I had served on. All the others had a fair scattering of two or three badge men who for one reason or another had no desire to become leading hands. I think that these old-timers were an essential ingredient in a crew's make-up. When tempers became frayed as they sometimes did, more often than not just a couple of words from these wise old seadogs would do more good than the sharp words from a leading hand's tongue. The very nature of the steam-easy attitude of these old-timers afforded a much valued stabilising effect on the mess-deck. Unfortunately the first two years of the war had taken its toll on so many of these men and they were now a luxury that could no longer be supplied.

With the boat now halfway through its trials there was still no change to the hostile atmosphere within the mess. Although this did not trigger off open conflict, the situation as it was, seemed far more menacing than if it had done so. How I would face up to this pressure during wartime patrols would remain to be seen.

One day when I entered the mess a few of the stokers were sitting round the table talking about the marvellous jobs they had in civvy street. One was a foreman bricklayer, and all the others claimed to have been charge-hands of one sort or another. For so many young people to have held such lucrative jobs seemed to me to be most unlikely.

'What did you do?' one of them asked me.

Half suspecting that this was yet again one of their loaded questions, I told them that I had not always been in the Navy, in fact up to the age of nineteen I too had earned a fair living as a painter and decorator.

Then sure enough came the next question, 'How would you set about painting a wall?' Although the question seemed so absurd I went to great pains to explain the rudiments of painting a wall. The fact that I had forgotten to mention that you lay off the paint with up and down brush strokes was quickly seized on by one of the former bricklayers.

'Oh,' he said, 'I was only a foreman bricklayer but I was always under the impression that you use up and down strokes.'

The smug smile on his face had said it all. Once again it seemed quite obvious that this small clique was happy to have scored points in their effort to undermine my authority.

If the boat was to survive the hazards of a wartime patrol, it was imperative that both man and machine should operate at the very highest standard of proficiency. In order to reach such standards the various exercises in which we were employed had to be repeated over and over again with monotonous regularity. I do not intend to dwell too much on the boat's working-up trials, so to keep it brief I can best describe the exercises under the following headings: deep diving, then torpedo and gunnery practice. To round off the programme the boat spent the last week or so acting as a clockwork mouse to anti-submarine patrol boats. This major exercise not only provided the training for the obvious participants, i.e. torpedo, gunnery and asdic operators, they also created a slipstream into which the entire crew would be drawn. Everybody in the crew had his part to play in it. It was only when the captain was satisfied that each man knew his job, would we then be ready to proceed on the boat's first patrol.

When all the training exercises had been brought to a satisfactory conclusion we departed from our safe haven in the Clyde and headed north towards Cape Wrath. The Pentland Firth being notorious for rough seas, where better to start a shakedown patrol? Unlike the other boats that I had served on, not a word of the captain's objective was passed along the grapevine and I could only guess that our patrolling area was somewhere of the coast of Norway. Although we made no contact with enemy shipping I suppose we could claim a certain amount of success, inasmuch as the adverse weather conditions gave the landlubbers a chance to find their sea-legs and to sharpen the eyes of the lookouts on the bridge. All things considered our young and immature crew seemed to shape up well for the task ahead.

During our trials the lounge bar in Dunoon's Crown Hotel had become a congenial retreat for most of the boat's crew. Should your rank be chief petty officer, able seaman or stoker, it did not seem to matter; so long as you had the cash to pay a round of drinks you were welcome to join the party. The object of the exercise was to down as many whisky and beer chasers as your body could hold without falling over.

With the boat now under sailing orders our last few hours ashore proved to be a humdinger. During the course of the evening we joined forces with some of the local talent who had dropped in from a nearby ballroom and after spending most of the evening in our company they decided to accompany us as far as the jetty which was a bus ride away at Sandbank. It seemed highly probable that these same lassies had waved goodbye to many other boat crews but nevertheless it was a good gesture and they did seem to show a genuine concern over our departure. After numerous goodbye kisses I stepped down into the motor boat just as it slid away from its berth and as I did so a choir-like chorus on the end of the jetty began to sing the old Scottish farewell ballad, 'We nae awar to bide awar'. As we moved towards the parent ship in the centre of the loch the noise of the motorboat engine's gradually overpowered the singing voices as the sight of the waving arms faded into the night.

A few hours later we left the Clyde and were on our way to join up with a large convoy. That to me was bad news. It meant that the trip out would be surface running all the way and I hated it. Not only was there the danger of being exposed to all and sundry, there was also the discomfort of being tossed about like a cork while trying to keep up with the speed of the convoy, and all this on a winter crossing in the Bay of Biscay. As I lay in my bunk trying to come to terms with the deafening roar of the engines, once again I had to face up to the stark realities of war as my thoughts flashed back to when I had left England bound for the Mediterranean. Only one of the four boats survived the first year, and dare I hope to be as lucky this time? The falling barometer was just a mere hint of the atrocious weather which lay in wait for us.

It was about the third night out when I took my turn to ditch the gash, then having discharged each bucketful over the side I stood momentarily looking aft towards the vicinity of the stokers' mess-deck. It looked as though in the midst of the raging sea, the whole stern was completely independent of the rest of the submarine. As I watched, it repeatedly took wide circular sweeps into the sky only to come crashing down into the angry sea with all the violence of a massive power hammer. How in hell do we live down there? I wondered.

While the heavy seas continued to pound away on our hull, conditions in the mess became intolerable. Most of the stokers seemed quite happy to stagger off watch and flop straight into their bunks so blocking off all access to the mess tables. The mess had been kept in total darkness for almost a week and the few of us who did want to sit down to a meal had no way of doing so. To add to the discomfort someone had used one of the buckets to vomit in and was careless enough to leave it untied. With the deck covered in slimy spew and tea leaves the place stank to high heaven. I thought the whole situation to be completely demoralising for all concerned. I began to question myself. Is it me? Do I expect too much from my inexperienced mess-mates? In other boats I had weathered storms equally bad but never with any other crew had living conditions become so unacceptable.

There is a very ancient axiom among seafarers. There is no ship as good as a sailor's last ship. As far as I was concerned the message provided by the old proverb contained more than a grain of truth that time. Had I been on any other boat I am sure the mess would have received a couple of friendly calls from the chief stoker. These visits were usually made after breakfast. He would ensure that everybody was on their feet and the mess scrubbed out each day and the bunks lowered from their chains. But for me there was no such back up. Being unable to find space in the mess I stepped through the bulkhead door into the motor room. I was sick and tired of being hemmed in by darkness for hours on end. It wasn't very comfortable sitting on the motor room bench but at least it was somewhere in the light where I could read. A few minutes later I was joined by the outside leading stoker.

'Have you seen that?' he asked. He pointed towards a notice which hung on the bulkhead door.

I answered, 'Yes I have seen it.' In large capitals it read, THE BLACK HOLE OF CALCUTTA. By then I could take no more.

'I think it is high time we had a clear-out,' I said to him.

I had just washed my feet after stepping out of my bunk into a pool of spew so I wasn't in a very happy mood. Having both agreed to do something about the situation we went back to the mess and switched on all the lights.

'Wake up your sleep is over, everybody wake up,' we shouted. We waited a minute or two before getting any response at all. It was only after continual shouting when a few bodies began to stir then gradually to the sound of half-muffled disapproving moans and groans as one by one they hit the deck Once again it was the same old few that remained defiant to the last by refusing to budge and so making it quite clear that they were openly challenging our authority.

The biggest culprit was a leading stoker who had just been made up and had joined the boat just prior to our departure from Scotland.

'Come on this means you too, you should be setting an example to these youngsters,' I shouted, yet still he did not stir. By then my patience was completely exhausted. 'I am giving you a direct order. Get out of your bunk,' I shouted. Giving me a string of abuse he then leapt to his feet like a shot from a cannon. From that moment on I knew that I had made an arch enemy.

Although the seas continued to be rough for the next two or three days, by the time we had reached Gibraltar we were at last beginning to settle into a much healthier routine. Each day the mess was scrubbed out and the bunks lowered from their chains while all three tables were set for meals. As the boat moved towards the shelter of the harbour all turbulence gradually subsided and much to the relief of all we were once again on an even keel. The effect of the sudden calm seemed almost uncanny; already my mess-mates were on their feet and moving about as lively as crickets. As their activities increase so did the tempo of conversation. For most of them it was their first chance to set foot on foreign soil and understandably a certain amount of excitement was only to be expected. As for myself I had seen it all before so it was no hardship to find out that I was duty watch. Apart from being a great place to buy duty-free gifts, Gibraltar had very little to offer in the way of entertainment, especially at night. The two or three bars in the main street so often became the stamping grounds where many young sailors fell foul of the shore patrols by becoming involved in punch-ups. At the time the patrol's kingpin was a giant of a man whose outsize uniform clung to his muscular hulk like a ballerina's leotard, and according to legend he was a bit of a musician. He loved to play tunes on matelot's skulls and for this reason all but the very foolish would try to steer well clear of trouble. For those of us who remained on board the evening found us fully engrossed in letter writing. In contrast to all the buffeting and the continual roar of the engines the only disturbance to hinder our concentration was the occasional tapping noise made by the sudden release of tension as the mooring springs relaxed with the moving tide. At times when submariners are obliged to return to the boat after an evening ashore, the cooling down period for over-exuberant shore-goers was a bone of contention with the night watchkeepers and judging by the rowdiness of the of the first few arrivals there would be no exception to the rule that night.

As they entered the mess I gathered together my pen pad, and ink with the intention of continuing my writing in the motor room. My past experience had taught me that it would be futile of me to expect to get any sleep for at least another two hours. While I was ready to forego my pre-watch sleep others were not so tolerant.

'Why don't you pipe down and give the watchkeepers a chance to sleep?' someone shouted.

Suddenly the senior leading hand appeared at the bulkhead door.

'I have had enough of this. It's pandemonium back there. I am going to fetch the coxswain,' he was shouting.

Almost on his heels my former adversary came charging past, sending me, the bottle of ink and writing paper flying on to the deck. In a flash I shot to my feet and let fly with both fists and in just a few seconds I gave him the most unmerciful hiding about the face and head. At no time did I ever feel pleased with myself for doing this, in fact I felt just the opposite. After the punch up I stood there shaking. In those few seconds I felt as though I had unleashed all my pent-up frustration and bitterness which like a cancer had been slowly eating away at my better nature.

Having retraced his steps during the commotion the senior leading hand stood in front of me shouting, 'What did you do that for? If I tell the coxswain now it will be you that is in trouble.'

'Do what you damn well like,' I snapped back at him.

However he decided to take no further action and returned to the mess where all its occupants by now had reached a state of subdued silence. It was too late for me to turn in so I sat in the motor room pondering over what had happened. If only the duty PO had been doing his job the incident would never had happened. Then at 0200 hours it was my turn to do a two hour stint on the casing as sentry. The bad feeling and clash in personalities which had with each day increased in magnitude almost from the first moment that I had joined the boat was only a whisper of the torment which was to follow. I got my first taste of what was to become a daily declaration on the following morning.

It all began when I saw him surveying his face in the mirror, 'I will get you for this,' he was saying. From then on I was subjected to continual threats. Given time I knew that he would recover from the bruising, but because he was a lot bigger than I, his pride and loss of face was something else to be reckoned with. By the time we had reached Port Said I was wishing that he would retaliate and give me a good hiding as I would have accepted anything to clear the air. In the morning after our arrival when I decided to give him a chance. The reason I chose that time was because the night before he had returned from shore leave full of booze and aggression when he once again reminded me that he had not forgotten. Being sick to death with his constant threats I lay there awake on my bunk waiting for morning to come. Then at 0700 hours I went to his bunk and shook him.

'Come on, there is no one about, it's you and me on the quay.' Who knows, I may have made it easy for him to even the score? But alas, his refusal to budge and the reply that he gave me only antagonised me more.

'I will get you in my time when you least expect it,' he snarled.

By now the rift between us had become common knowledge throughout the boat. So it was no surprise to me when the engineer officer asked both of us to join him in the control room for a chat. He began by telling us that he was very concerned about the animosity between us which was obviously bad for the morale of the stokers' branch as a whole. He then asked us to let bygones be bygones and shake hands. This we both agreed would be best for all and did so. For a couple of days we were all nice and friendly although I must admit I was treating our new relationship with the same amount of caution with which I would woo a tigress. It wasn't long before my suspicion was confirmed. It was tot time the next day when sitting at the table at the far end of the mess I heard him say to one of his cronies,

'If he thinks that he has got away with it, he has another think coming.'

From my past experiences in the North Sea I always feared daylight running on the surface and now that we had entered the Indian Ocean my observations could only enhance my suppressed awareness of how vulnerable a submarine could be to a surprise attack from aircraft. We were heading east about three days out from Aden when I took advantage of the rare opportunity of viewing the horizon by daylight. Although the sea was calm I was

amazed by the number of tracks which were left by the
wake of the ships, all of which seemed to have taken
different routes leaving criss-cross patterns which were
spread out in all directions as far as the eye could see and
yet there was not a ship in sight. If we have to crash dive
because of attacking aircraft surely such a trail as I had just
seen would be a dead give-away to our exact position I
thought. Of course the lookouts had long since been aware
of the potential hazard resulting from this phenomena but
as for myself I had felt much more secure before I had
gained this knowledge, then having seen for myself I knew
that it would be some time before I could accept the danger
with such apparent fortitude as they.

Our arrival in Trincomalee coincided with that of the
Tantalus. As I looked towards her I could see one of my old
ship-mates standing on the casing. He was a young New
Zealander who had served on the *Thrasher* with me.

'How are you doing, Digger?' I shouted.

'I am very well. We are on our way to the UK. Don't
you wish that you were with us?' he taunted. Obviously he
had been informed that we were about to start on our first
Far East patrol.

So I called to him, 'What are the ash-cans like out here?'

As I expected Stoker Berrick was just as defiant as ever,
'Those bloody Japs don't know how to depth-charge, they
missed us by miles,' he shouted.

The same evening I saw another of the *Thrasher*'s crew,
this time it was Stoker York. He was leaning over the bows
of the *Tantalus* holding what I thought to be a hand-line.

'What's the fishing like, Yorky?' I called.

'I am not fishing I have a magnet tied to the end, I am
trying to find a watch that I dropped over the side,' he
answered.

Then forming two rings with my forefingers and
thumbs I held them to my eyes and shouted, 'I think you

have really flipped your lid now.'

His broad grin and expressive gesture was enough to tell me that he had not forgotten our little skylarks on the *Thrasher*, when during our engine room watches we used to amuse ourselves by hooting to each other like night owls. That in itself should have been reason enough to be entered on the psychiatrist's short list, but to try and fish a wristwatch from the middle of the Indian Ocean, surely he must have had at least one leg inside the loony bin.

After a brief stay in Trincomalee we turned our bows south towards the coastline off Sumatra where, after relentless searching for a sizeable prize, our captain had to satisfy our entitlement to fly the Jolly Roger by sinking nothing larger than a caique. Although these vessels were small, large numbers of them were used to transport valuable rubber for the Japs. As long as the operation would not jeopardise our chances of sinking larger targets these small boats were considered to be fair game for an idle gun's crew to exercise its power of destruction. Before this was done our captain invited its crew of three to take refuge on board our submarine and having no other option they did so. Surprisingly these marvellous sailors of Indonesian origin were very young. At first they looked terrified as they stayed huddled together obviously thinking that they would be shot. Because of the language barrier it took us a long time to explain to them that they would be perfectly safe in our custody. One of our problems was that of feeding them, the only food that seemed agreeable to them was the old submariner's standby, herrings in tomato sauce, and they scoffed away on these until the juice ran out of their ears.

Using all sorts of sign language we tried to communicate with the threesome. We all felt so sorry for them, none more so than our gunlayer who had the nerve to ask the captain to put them on another caique and let them go. The same night the captain ordered the gunlayer to bring our visitors to the bridge.

Addressing him the captain said, 'Gunlayer your request has been granted. You can discharge the prisoners to the care of the captain of this other caique.'

When this was done the captain asked, 'Does that make you happy now gunlayer?'

All was well until four hours later when a signal from another submarine which was several miles away was pinned to our notice board. It read something like this. 'Have intercepted and sunk caique, Have taken aboard six prisoners, three of whom speak very good English – herrings in – herrings in.'

The remaining six weeks on patrol consisted of little more than sweat, prickly heat and sheer boredom but all of this was soon forgotten when we arrived at Fremantle in Western Australia. Almost as soon as the fore-hatch was opened a churn of milk was placed on the casing. This unexpected token of friendship was made available to us with the compliments of the people of Perth. Such generosity was just a forerunner of the welcome that we received ashore. Almost everybody aboard was taken into somebody's home. Three months had passed since. we left Scotland and after spending all that time cramped together with fifteen other bodies in the after-ends, five days up country gave me a taste of Australian life in the outback. I felt like a caged wild bird which had just been freed. Back in Fremantle minor repairs to our boat were already put into operation and in less than three weeks we were heading north towards the Lombok Straits. Although this was to be one of my longest patrols of the war, it was also a negative one. Had it not been for two spine-chilling experiences, to my mind this patrol might never have happened.

It began one morning during a periscope watch in our

first designated patrol area. We had been submerged for about four hours and as I lay on my bunk the dead silence was broken by the whirring noise of a salvo of torpedoes. Suddenly the still bodies of the off-watch stokers sprang to life, almost everyone together asked the same question. 'What's that?'

'Don't worry, they were torpedoes. They have missed us,' I said.

Almost immediately the tannoy blurted out, 'Shut off for deep diving, shut all bulkhead doors, silent routine.' The cat and mouse game that followed continued for twelve hours or more during which time neither submarine could ascertain with accuracy the other's exact position. It was well after nightfall before our captain decided that it was safe enough to surface, but almost as soon as the lookouts had positioned themselves on the bridge a voice screamed down the voicepipe, 'Dive, dive, dive.' As the first lookout hit the control room deck, 'Torpedoes,' he cried out. Within a few seconds the message was passed to the after-ends. With both main motors switched to 'group up, full ahead' the boat reached the depth of eighty feet so it seemed safe to assume that the Japs had failed in their second attempt to blow us to kingdom come. For the next two hours we and our adversaries became engaged in a deadly contest of cunning as each submarine tried to line up its enemy for the final kill. Having made fruitless efforts to establish the Japs' submerged position our captain decided it was time to try our luck on the surface once again. After careful sweeps using hydrophone and peri-scope, we broke surface. Then for a few agonising seconds we waited fully expecting to have to crash dive again. Suddenly the telegraphs rang 'stop main motors, in both engine clutches'. Then 'full ahead' both main engines. The tension that had built up slowly began to ease with the realisation that these orders indicated that our captain now thought it would be expedient for our boat to show a fluffy tail and get to hell out of the area.

For another twenty days or so we continued to hunt down the enemy ships along the coast of Java but despite the crew's desire to contribute to shortening the war, all our efforts proved to be in vain. Our boat was now eight months into commission yet once again we had to return to our base in Perth to suffer the humiliation of still being unqualified to fly the Jolly Roger. Unlike the Yanks who had two crews to each of their boats thus allowing them to take it in turn to do their patrols, we were stuck with just the one crew and all too soon our stay in harbour was coming to an end. The final adjustments were made to ensure the boat's sea worthiness by berthing it on the slipway at Fremantle. Once the boat was high and dry access to the external hull fittings became readily available for cleaning and repair work. It was during our last full day in harbour that this work was done.

At 0830 the following morning I returned to Fremantle after an all-night leave in Perth. I discovered that the boat had left the slipway and had taken up a position alongside the parent ship and I was about to enter the crew space when I was stopped by the ERA who had been responsible for the repairs made to the hull fittings the night before. He was standing just above the forward machine space hatch. He told me that he had been pushed for time when refitting the main ballast pump hull valve. This valve controls the sea inlet and has an orifice six or eight inches diameter. It is located on the lower part of the machine space on the port side. I would estimate the inlet to be about twelve foot below the waterline. The valve box itself was secured to the hull by four three-quarter inch studs and the threaded bores which housed the studs were set almost equidistantly round the valves circumference. The ERA explained to me that he had only enough time to get one of these studs into position. He then asked me to do him a favour by replacing the other three studs so as to secure the valve for deep diving. Although it was not my job and not realising the forthcoming implications I agreed to help him out. I had no problem screwing the second stud into position but when it came to the third one only half the orifice of the stud's housing could be seen. As for the fourth stud the orifice was completely hidden. After giving the valve a closer look I realised that it had been replaced ninety degrees out of position thereby making it impossible to secure the other two studs. This meant that three-quarters of the valve's circumference would have been subjected to enormous pressures once the boat had submerged beyond periscope depth. If this condition had been allowed to remain one could well imagine what could happen.

Realising the danger I went to tell the ERA what I thought. I could hardly believe what was happening when he adopted the attitude, 'Leave it alone and it will go away.' By midday the boat had shipped aboard all stores for a two month patrol and as each hour passed I was becoming more and more worried. Although I had made several attempts to make the ERA realise the danger if we were to proceed on patrol without first rectifying the fault, he still ignored my plea to report the matter to the engineer officer. As time drew near for our departure I had worked myself almost to the point of panic. In desperation I went along to the ERA's mess where they were all sitting down at the table. I asked them as mess-mates to try and persuade the culprit to own up to the mistake that he had made, but to my astonishment they all told me that they did not want to get involved. By this time my frustration had become overwhelming and I could not help thinking that I was surrounded by idiots. Surely these men had enough training to realise that to proceed on patrol like this would spell complete disaster to the boat with all its crew. In just a few hours we would be doing our trim dive and if this valve was exposed to any depth at all the pressure would snap off the studs like dry twigs thus leaving the largest compartment in the boat to the mercy of the sea.

Late that afternoon I paid another visit to the forward machine space. I suppose at the back of my mind I had hoped that the ERA would by some miracle have found a way to remedy his mistake but how this could be done without going back to the slipway wouldn't bear thinking about. Imagine my surprise when I saw all the studs in place. But to me it did not seem possible that the valve could be taken off and replaced while the boat was still afloat. However further scrutiny revealed to me that the studs had been sawn in half, then a nut had been screwed on one end of each half and just placed in the vacant holes round the edged of the flange. In short the job was so bodged up that it would hardly be worthy of the efforts of a six-year-old boy.

After picking the studs out with my fingers, I thought that was the last straw and reported my findings to the chief ERA His reaction was alarming. He just shrugged his shoulders and said, 'It's nothing to do with me, I'm in charge of the engine room.'

To me it was frightening; no matter where I turned nobody wanted to know. As our departure time drew ever nearer I began to think of my own safety I knew in my own mind that I would never venture so much as a trim dive in the boat. I must admit that I had even thought of jumping ship if only to save my own skin. Thankfully common sense prevailed when I attacked the ERA for the last time.

'If you don't do something about the valve I will,' I screamed out.

I was shaking in temper. At the time of this confrontation he was sitting in his mess in company with the chief and the other three ERAs. After shouting so loud I couldn't understand why the engineer and the other officers in the wardroom paid no attention to the commotion, the wardroom being adjacent to the ERAs' mess. It was a mystery that someone was not asking questions. It wasn't until the chief ERA made a gesture by nodding his head before the outside ERA made any attempt to move from the table. He then reacted to my demand with a sneer and addressed me in a sarcastic tone, 'Okay pal.'

Such was his reply that his words almost made me feel that it was I who was the guilty party. I waited for him to make a move towards the engineer officer who was still in the wardroom. Then cursing like mad I went back to my mess, but not before I had made certain that he had informed the officer. It was a great relief to me when I saw both of them making hasty tracks towards the forward AMS. It was late in the afternoon before arrangements could be made with the Australians to authorise a last minute docking on the slipway. I knew that the boat would be late starting out on its patrol and someone would have to answer for it. After hasty repairs it was almost dusk before our boat slid past the boom defence barrier. Still feeling uneasy about the outcome of my discovery I paid another visit to the AMS to see if I could find any evidence of the sawn off studs but unfortunately this was to no avail, I then went to the engine room vice bench to look for iron filings only to find both vice and bench were as clean as new pins.

With the sun now dropping below the horizon our boat began to respond to the swell of the open sea. The helmsman was ordered to set a northerly course which in three or four days would take us into the Timor Sea. We knew that once again our patrol area would be the Java Sea. It was therefore clear to all aboard that we would soon be facing the hazard of penetrating the Lombok Straits. The rip tide which pours down through the narrows made it necessary for us to make our run through the Straits on the surface at night and even then the tide was so strong that our progress would be slow. Be it the night's darkest hour, there was always the risk of being spotted by a very efficient enemy whose constant vigilance was respected by every lookout on the bridge. However the risk did pay off because after an undetected dash through the Straits we later contacted the boat's most promising target to date.

It was 12th July, 1945, when the captain's order for gun action echoed through the boat's tannoy system. Quickly word was spread throughout the boat that the periscope watchkeeper had sighted a convoy consisting of a floating dock which was being towed by a vessel which carried the only gun which could have been a threat to us. After the first round or so the threat was rendered harmless when our gunlayer scored a direct hit. He then turned the gun on a submarine which had opened fire on us but whose shells were falling short due to being outranged. With the submarine out of the way we continued to fire into the side of the floating dock but after what must have been thirty rounds the damn thing still remained afloat. If my memory serves me correctly the captain only broke off action after an unsuccessful attempt to sink it by firing two torpedoes into its flank. That was the only time in the war that I was never threatened by depth-charges after a major sinking. Recent research revealed to me that the submarine that we sank was one belonging to the Dutch Navy but was commandeered by the Japs who used it to spot allied activity in the region.

Slowly the days turned to weeks and not until August did we the crew feel any relief from the relentless boredom which at times became more dreaded than the obvious dangers that we faced up to. News that the atom bomb had been dropped on Hiroshima sent a wave of excitement through the boat which at first had the effect of a powerful stimulant injection. Our first concern was that it would shorten the war, but after a short while a sixth sense seemed to chill my bones. What kind of a monster had we unleashed to cause such suffering to mankind? Although there was little known about the true measure of destruction to life and limb I think everybody knew that the casualties would be horrendous. So far it seemed that the annihilation of Hiroshima had not brought the desired effect of undermining the Japanese resolve to continue fighting the war.

As the days passed our recall to base seemed as far away as ever. It was not until the second bomb exploded on Nagasaki when we received the long-awaited news that the Japanese had surrendered. With this news we had the order to cease fire and return to Fremantle. The possibility of meeting up with isolated pockets of resistance while making our surface run down to Lombok Straits kept the lookouts on full alert. Evidently the garrison guarding the Straits was one of the groups which over the past few days had displayed defiance by ignoring orders given by their own high command to lay down their arms and surrender.

Prior to reaching the narrows the captain ordered the control room watchkeeper to bring a huge Union Jack up on to the bridge. With the periscope raised to its full height the flag was secured to it. With the Jap airbase almost on top of us I thought that it was an extremely unwise move. Almost at once Jap planes were on top of us and I had hardly reached my diving station before the first stick of depth-bombs exploded all round us. At the time my job was to operate the main ballast pump which was tucked away in the corner of the forward auxiliary machine space. It was a very isolated place to be while being repeatedly depth-charged and being stripped to the waist our bare torsos had become the target for the cork chippings and ice chilling beads of condensation which were flying from the deck and bulkheads like bullets with the violence of each explosion.

After a short while I said to the young stoker who was down there with me, 'There is no point in two of us getting soaked and there is no room for you to help me in any way, go and sit on top of the hatchway and have a chat with the seamen.' At least it was dry up there and much more comfortable.

The south-flowing rip tide through the Lombok Straits which hindered us on our outward voyage was now in our favour because it was now possible to reach a much higher speed submerged than we could otherwise achieve. Thus we were able to reach deeper water before the planes had time to home in on us again. After it was all over young Taffy and I went back to the mess to join in with the chat which always helped to unwind the pent up nerves after such an ordeal. The wisdom over the decision to taunt the Japs by flying the oversize Union Jack came under a lot of criticism because having survived the war so far, it was almost curtains for us all. After being submerged for an hour or so we made steady progress towards the open sea. After a thorough search of the skies through the periscope and seeing no sign of enemy planes the captain decided it was safe to surface. From then on we continued our run back to Fremantle without further harassment. Soon after the boat had been secured alongside the parent ship some of the stokers opened up the after-hatch and climbed on to the casing to take a breath of fresh air. The remaining half a dozen including myself bustled around the mess collecting mess-traps together ready to transfer them to our allocated mess on the parent ship.

I suddenly became aware of the engineer officer standing just inside the entrance to the motor room. Calling the outside leading stoker and myself to one side, he said to the former, 'You will be pleased to know that your promotion to Petty Officer has been approved.' Then turning to me he said, 'Your promotion I have turned down on the grounds that I do not consider you to be suitable for advancement.'

Feeling thoroughly disgusted I trembled as I tried to regain my composure. As if that wasn't enough he then told me that the boat was returning to the UK and that I would be drafted to the parent ship from that afternoon. Although my contempt towards this officer was never greater than it was at that moment, I somehow managed to conceal it. To me it seemed beyond all reasoning that anybody could be so blind. The engineer's departure left the remaining members of the mess numb with silence and I have no recollection of being offered any condolences. Perhaps I was too upset to notice it. It took all my strength to hide my emotions but I was determined not to show how much I was hurt. For the time being I would just have to console myself with the relief that the war was over and I would make the best of the remaining two years I had yet to serve. In sheer disgust for all concerned I remained silent as I collected my personal belongings and walked out of the mess leaving them to stew in their own juice. I don't think any of them realised how near they were to becoming statistics on a long list of submarine casualties, some of which was known to be caused by sheer ignorance.

After a good soaking under the shower I waited for the words, 'Liberty men fall in on the quarterdeck,' to be piped over the ship's tannoy. I was thinking that a few hours ashore and a few bottles of beer would relieve the frustration that remained within me. All I wanted to do was to get away from it all. As I stood in the ranks waiting for the officer of the watch inspection I immediately spotted the engineer officer standing by the quarterdeck just inside the covered way. I particularly noticed his attire. Although the boat had been alongside for most of the day he was still dressed in his shabby engine room jacket and cap.

How strange, I thought. Why is he standing there? For an instant I thought how worried he looked. Had he found out the truth about the valve? Then suddenly our eyes met and as they did I quickly turned away, but that fleeting glance was long enough for him to have read my thoughts.

'Shattock, I want to speak to you,' he called out.

After walking over to where he was standing, I stopped and saluted. 'Yes sir,' I answered.

'It's nothing personal you understand,' he said. For a brief second I stood there motionless, then giving him a mocking smile, I lied, 'That's all right, I am not in the least worried sir, forget about it.'

For the next few days I was tormented by the feeling that I had suffered a grave injustice and how I had allowed myself to be used as a scapegoat was beyond all comprehension. By then I had dismissed all thought of presenting the facts to higher authorities as past experience had taught me not to expect any corroboration from the ERAs on the boat, all of whom knew some of the facts. Such evidence as the sawn-off studs had long since been destroyed making me feel that I had little chance of obtaining a fair hearing. A sense of loyalty was perhaps an attribute which had been instilled into me at a very early age but had now taken a severe knock. I had always tried to do the right thing by others and I always expected a reciprocal response. I suppose such illusions stems from being young and naive but today having drifted a fair way through the sea of life, I would approach a similar situation with much more caution because in terms of pride this was a costly lesson to me.

After a brief spell in the parent ship's spare crew I left Fremantle on the submarine *Taurus*. Our mission was to show the flag in a few ports around Australia and later to the islands in the Pacific Ocean. The numerous farewell parties given by my friends ashore had for a time helped me to forget the shattering blow to my self-esteem. Such diversions came to an end almost as soon as the *Taurus* put to sea. Although the atmosphere in the stokers' mess seemed friendly enough I was soon to discover an aura of discontentment and unrest among the lower-deck person-nel. This was the perfect climate for me to ponder over the injustice that I had endured. The bitter brew was seething over and over inside me and I knew that a forthcoming eruption would be inevitable.

The stage was set when we reached Adelaide, South Australia. At the time there were no fewer than a dozen men doing punishment. Most of these had been for minor offences but there were three stokers on a much more serious charge. Between them they had broken into the wine and spirit locker in the wardroom and subsequently got stoned out of their minds. They wrecked a large lampshade which was adorned with pictures of beautiful maidens, then for good measure they emptied bottles of ink all over the bed linen of the first lieutenant's bunk. Not surprisingly all three were placed under close arrest awaiting such time when they could be dealt with by someone with higher authority than the captain.

After being restricted to the boundaries within the hull of a submarine it is always a pleasure to set foot on terra firma. The good food and comfortable surroundings that were provided by the Australian Navy shore base was welcomed as an extra bonus, but not for me, because once again I was left out on a limb. While the whole boat's crew was living it up ashore I was put in charge of the prisoners and was given instructions that on no account were they to leave the boat. Arrangements were made for me to collect our meals from a hut on the dockside.

The fun started when I had to inform them that some-one had stolen the dinners. The only way that I could quell their protest was by promising to somehow obtain a few rolls which of course had to be washed down with lashings of beer. This I managed to do by employing the services of a young lad who had been seen hanging about the dockside. Giving him an empty potato sack and ample dough from my own pocket I waited half-expecting him to never return from the nearest bar which was just a stone's throw from the dockyard gate but this he did and so I managed to keep them quiet until teatime. At 1600 hours I went over to the hut to collect the food for tea only to find that the same thing had happened again.

Having no means to communicate with someone of higher authority I went back to the prisoners and said, 'That's it. We are all going ashore.'

My charges needed little encouragement. We all sauntered out of the dockyard and into the bar across the road. That was the last thing that I remembered until I woke up on my bunk late that evening. By then I had a hazy recollection of someone telling me that I too was now under close arrest. With the duty watch now on board for the night there were plenty of hands to stop further trouble. The relief guard was given the orders to inform the coxswain as soon as I regained consciousness. Within a minute or so a messenger was standing over my bunk telling me to report to the coxswain immediately.

It wasn't until the next day that I became aware of what followed. From a flood of verbal obscenities the coxswain's runner somehow managed to decode my reply. In short I refused to move from my bunk. That evening when I finally came to my senses, one of the prisoners informed me that they felt sorry for me, so between them they lifted me into an old discarded wheelbarrow and brought me back to the boat. They said that because I was time-serving I had a lot more to loose than they did. At 0900 hours the next morning, a much more subdued leading stoker stood before the first lieutenant being asked to explain the slight misdemeanour. I was not surprised to find that my offence was too grave for him to handle and so I was put on captain's report. The captain was in no hurry to administer what he judged to be the appropriate punishment.

The passing weeks gave me plenty of time to think about the consequences. How on earth could I get out of this one? If I could only conjure up some plausible excuse perhaps the captain would go easy on me but startling new evidence had come to light which brought the curtains down on that idea. I had now became aware that the captain knew all about my escapade. While my mess-mates seemed highly amused because the prisoners were courteous enough to taxi me back to the boat in the builder's wheel-barrow I wondered if this sporting gesture would be appreciated by the captain. It seemed quite a while before the dreaded day arrived and by then the boat had moved round to the next port of call, Melbourne.

It was soon after the boat had berthed when a message blurted out over the boat's tannoy, 'Leading Stoker Shattock report to the control room.' My stomach turned over, this is it, now I'm in for the high jump, I thought to myself.

The coxswain gave me a few minutes to change into full uniform during which time the boat's crew was ordered to fall in on the quayside. I was then escorted ashore and marched to a spot in front of the captain. The prospect of what was about to happen to me seemed gloomy enough but when I glanced to one side I was in for another shock. At the time the boat was about to be opened to visitors and I became fully aware that I was about to become a spectacle before all eyes of a crowd who had gathered nearby. When the coxswain read out the charge I stood motionless as my mind seemed to blank out the reality of what was happening.

Although I had planned to make excuses for myself, when it came to the crunch I elected to say nothing and I could not believe my luck when the captain said, 'You will be deprived of one good conduct badge.' I had quite expected to be sent to prison with the others.

Chapter Eleven

Resentment

My story so far has been a dialogue of events which happened many years ago but nevertheless such memories remain embedded in my mind as the happenings of today, but for reasons which I fail to understand the remaining episode, although factual, the exact sequence of some of the events now evades me.

With the war just a few weeks behind me I was trying to come to terms with the topsy-turvy routine which was caused by the adjustments to submarine crews which had been made in order to comply with orders from the Admiralty that all time expired men and hostilities only personnel were to be released forthwith. This news only added to my frustration, would I ever get home I asked myself? As far as I was concerned this announcement caused bad feelings of resentment and restlessness. With my mind completely absorbed with the burning desire to celebrate the end of the war with my family at home in the UK. That much I thought I had earned but was unfairly deprived of the opportunity. Up to this time I had no false illusions about myself. After my recent fiasco when I was put in charge of the three prisoners, it would take a very brave commanding officer to favour the likes of myself with a recommendation for promotion, so with these thoughts in mind I could no longer hope to benefit by serving a second term in the Royal Navy. From then on my remaining two years was going to be all fun and games.

Having made a few runs ashore I soon became insolvent. In order to satisfy my lust for good times I was forced to devise various means to replenish my finances. However the problem was soon solved when I met the crew of a barracuda fishing vessel, I soon discovered that they were prepared to pay a good price for a tin of shag tobacco. It so happened that in a locker under one of the bunks in the mess there was a stash of the stuff which had long been forgotten about. It was simply packed away waiting for some entrepreneur to make a pay day. The reason no one wanted it was because it was South African tobacco which we all judged to be inferior to the Virginian, it wasn't until my mess-mates discovered the source of my recent wealth that anybody made claim to it. Then they all wanted a share in the spoils.

'Some hopes,' I said. After a thorough search in the other spare lockers I came across a promising supply of tinned sardines and herrings in tomato sauce, although we the crew had become sick of the sight of them it would seem that the people ashore would welcome them as a luxury. So once again that which had been regarded as rubbish would soon become a valuable commodity when fraternising with the local talent. Such assets were often used as a ticket for uphomers. That was an expression that soon was to become part and parcel of every day conversation on the mess-deck.

I remember one particular Sunday a few of us providers met up with a youthful-looking widow and her three attractive daughters. At the time drinking hours were very restricted in parts of Australia, so it came as no surprise to be invited up home. All the liquor stores were closed so we hailed a taxi and persuaded the driver to take us to one of the vineyards on the outskirts of the city. When we arrived there we were met by a man of Italian descent who offered quite a lot of opposition during our haggling over the price. To our smug satisfaction it all ended well in our favour when just for a few pounds we walked away with a sack full of cheap plonk, then once home we settled down to a night of debauchery.

As the evening wore on gatecrashers swarmed into the house from all directions, with the building almost bursting at its seams bodies were lying all over the place. As each of us jostled to gain favour from a particular partner I sensed a growing amount of rivalry among the ladies. The trouble started when our widowed hostess was cast aside to make room for a voluptuous blonde who had recently gained entry to the orgy. With a large number of unopened wine bottles still standing on the kitchen table something had to be done to stop the party from breaking up and so it was left to yours truly to try his expert hand at consoling the distraught lady. I never did get the chance to compare notes with the guy who ran off with the blonde bombshell but I would have taken odds that I did better. Mummy was most appreciative of my soothing. My biggest surprise happened the next morning when I staggered into the kitchen to get a glass of water, as I passed through the doorway my attention was drawn to the sounds of grunting and groaning coming from beneath the kitchen table. I could hardly believe my eyes when I gazed down at the floor, as I did so a somewhat distorted replica of the human form crawled out from beneath it. As he emerged into full vision I recognised him to be none other than the cab driver who had taken us there on the previous day.

'Well since you are still here,' I said, 'you may as well drive us back to the boat.' From my position in the back of the cab I was able to study the reflection of the driver's mournful face through the driving mirror.

'You look worried,' I said to him.

He then told me that he was in a lot of trouble because it

was not his cab but that of a company who would not appreciate his twenty-four hours' absence from the taxi ranks.

'For sure it's the bullet for me,' he said.

I suppose we should have felt sorry for the poor devil, but instead we were laughing all the way back to the quay. That was his problem we thought. Over the next few weeks every port of call that we visited offered the same hospitality, parties and romances were springing up from all directions, the latter being very short term indeed.

Our visit to Hobart, Tasmania I could never forget. We had only been there a few days when my duties required my presence in the fore-ends, as I passed the seamen's mess I looked in at the entrance when my eyes feasted on what could only be described as a delightful scene, presenting depravity in its lowest form. Extending lengthways above the centre of the mess-deck table a fourteen foot clothesline had been strung from bulkhead to bulkhead. The line was adorned with several pairs of ladies' knickers covering the entire length. Someone with a warped sense of humour evidently kept count of his conquests. The fact that there was very little overhead room for a clothesline seemed of no consequence. When the lads sat round the table at mealtimes they seemed quite happy with the frills dangling in the soup.

On another occasion we had open day in the boat. Such an event always proved to be the ideal time to find a girlfriend because the ladies were always keen to acquire first-hand knowledge about the mysterious workings of a submarine, at least, that is what they used to tell us. During the afternoon one of the sailors was showing his girlfriend round the boat when his mess-mate suggested that he should show her the gun-tower.

'It's nice and quiet up there,' he said. But what he didn't say was that in the morning he had been up there with a can of red oxide and a paintbrush. Both parties seemed so keen to enjoy a little privacy, and they made no bones about climbing the ladder and opening the hatch only to disappear from sight before closing it behind them. It was some time before they emerged from their hideout. Seemingly they were completely unaware of the state they were in when they climbed down the ladder into a crowded control room, while the people gawped at the pair, the muttering comments and giggles must have warned them that something was wrong. From behind, the girl looked like a Red Indian squaw.

Before we set sail for Tasmania, rumour had it that the female species outnumbered that of the male by five to one but even with this knowledge, it still didn't prepare us to cope with such blatant prowess of so many flirtatious women. There was room for all of us, even the ugly ones. We stayed in Hobart for about five days. There were at least six submarines all berthed line ahead alongside the wharf. The last night there I found myself watch aboard and everyone in the boat knowing the lads would be enjoying a good time ashore, there was no offers for substitution so I had to settle for a restless evening just sitting in the mess with nothing to do but ponder over the fun and games that I was missing. It was round about midnight when I decided to take a stroll along the quay. I was some distance away from my boat when I stopped to have a chat with one of the sentries about five boats astern of us. He told me that while he was on watch he had been highly amused by the antics of several sailors and their girlfriends, the latter being unable to bear the thought of their boyfriends' departure the next morning decided to spend the night with them in a huge disused warehouse which stood adjacent to the wharf. Apparently during the last hour every now and again a couple would creep along the wharf, the sailor would leave his girlfriend by the entrance to the warehouse and go down to his boat and return to her side with a mattress off one of the bunks. The sentry told me that there were at least a dozen couples bedded down inside the warehouse.

Early next morning we were once again bound for the open sea. With our bow pointing north-east our next port of call was to be Sydney, New South Wales. A few days after the boat had docked near to the Circular Quay, the ship's postman came bursting into the mess saying that he had received some enlightening news from Hobart. The news had arrived in the form of Hobart's local newspaper. As we clambered over each other to get a glimpse of it we found that the whole of the front and centre pages had been dedicated to portray a sordid account of rude awakenings of several couples in the disused warehouse during the night before we left. Apparently the police with reporters raided the building soon after my chat with the sentry. While the identity of the sailors had not been disclosed, one of the girlfriends had a hell of a lot of explaining to do. It was alleged that while she was on her honeymoon a Sydney bride had mislaid her husband for twenty-four hours. The reporter had written a most titillating account of the truly blushing bride's compromising position with a sailor who had eagerly accepted the role as a stand-in lover for the night. There beneath the broad beam of torchlight the completely nude couple were caught well at it.

Australian hospitality continued to overwhelm us during our stay in Sydney, what with the parties and night-clubs we almost welcomed the opportunity to get away from it for a week. The chance came when one of the local charities offered the whole crew a week's paid holiday in the Blue Mountains. Speaking for myself I was always reluctant when it came to accepting handouts, or what old salts call 'grippos'. However I did learn a lesson in Adelaide a month earlier. As soon as we docked there one of the local dignitaries came aboard and told us that a ladies' church organisation had asked the whole crew to accompany them on a picnic party up in the hills on the outskirts of the city. Now you can imagine after crossing the Great Australian Bight during a terrific gale, the last thing that a submariner would wish for was to play games of ring-a-roses with a lot of church-going fuddy-duddies. Such were our thoughts that none of us would volunteer to go. Under pressure from the captain, the coxswain forced us to accept the invitation.

Having been paraded on the quay we were split into groups of three and ushered into waiting cars which were lined up one behind the other. As the cars cruised through the city it was follow my leader, with horns sounding off all the way to the hills. While the ladies were obviously enjoying the din we sailors stared into each other's faces not knowing whether to laugh or cry. We felt like children being taken on a Sunday school outing. We had not gone far before our bomb happy gunlayer voiced our disapproval in no uncertain terms.

I cringed in my seat when he blurted out, 'We were forced to come on this outing.'

Well the poor woman behind the wheel became so disorientated because of this outburst that she almost ran the car into a ditch. Eventually the whole fleet of cars veered off the road into a huge parkland area. With all cars being placed at a respectable distance from each other our hostess opened up the boot of her car and proceeded to spread a tablecloth on the lush green while we looked on like timid children. Then suddenly the gunlayer started off again.

'We would much sooner go back to the city,' he taunted.

By now the two ladies had reached the end of their tether. 'Would you like us to take you back there?' they asked.

They looked so bewildered that I felt utterly ashamed.

As the others settled down to feast we three climbed back into the car. With a very distraught lady at the wheel we drove on to the highway and headed back to the city. As we approached the city centre our driver turned to us and asked where would you like to be dropped off.

'Anywhere near to a bar,' we answered. Then came the sting.

'Oh this is South Australia. You will not find a bar open anywhere today because it's Sunday.'

How right she was, we spent hours treading the desolate streets looking for somewhere to quench our dry throats, but we may as well have been in the middle of the Nullabor Desert. Then to rub salt in our wounds, when we arrived back on board we were greeted by the rest of our crewmates who were overflowing with elation. They had a whale of a time, and the games that they played were not ring-a-roses. So with these thoughts still fresh in my mind I was not about to refuse this latest offer, that of a free week's holiday in the Blue Mountains.

A few days later a coach took half the crew to Parramatta railway station to catch the early morning train to the mountains. I and two other stokers were given an address in Katoomba. The house belonged to a lady who proved to be a most hospitable hostess for the duration of our stay with her. As I recall Katoomba at that time could hardly be regarded as so much as a small town set in the heart of a vast forest area high in the mountains. The house itself was of wooden structure thus very prone to fire, hence the lady's concern as to whether we smoked. When we answered that we all did, she warned us to be very careful. So as to quell her fears of setting fire to her home we assured her that we would not smoke in the house. Since that time I have heard of so many disasters in those forest areas. The surrounding scenery was something to be marvelled at, for us this was going to be shore leave with a difference. Pedal cycles and horses were made available so visits to the beauty spots took preference to our usual pastime such as drinking. Instead we chose to abandon our nautical inclinations in favour of those expected of country gentlemen.

Each morning after a hearty breakfast of eggs and bacon, we would cycle along to the local riding school the proprietor of which was blessed with the name of Donoghue. A fitting name for a stable, I thought. When I asked him if he was related to the great Steve, he didn't claim to have been so. On our first meeting he asked us if we had any experience of horses. I told him that it was years since I had been on the back of a horse, as for my colleagues they both claimed to be experts. After helping us to saddle up he gave us a few tips and sent us trekking through the forest glade. The others seemed to manage well on their mounts but my bloody thing was so docile he could hardly put one foot before the other.

The further I took him from the stable the slower he walked. After a couple of days my colleagues had completely mastered the art of riding, as for myself I was always the one that was left trailing behind. Thinking that I was ready to try my skill on something more lively I persuaded one of the lads to change mounts with me. The horse that I chose was a fine-looking animal that stood at least two hands higher than my one. As I mounted him he leapt forward with all the enthusiasm of a racehorse. He continued the gallop for a quarter mile when suddenly he took a right turn and made straight for a garden entrance, luckily the gate was open. Imagine my horror as it went charging towards a large greenhouse which was only a few yards inside the opening. Then to make matters worse, a large fat lady ran out between the galloping horse and the greenhouse. She was completely clothed in white and stood her ground only inches away from the glass, I instinctively pulled hard on the reins as the woman stood there waving her large apron in front of the horse. For me it was a terrifying experience as the horse reared several times on its hind legs, bringing its front hooves crashing down missing the lady by inches. After I dismounted it took me a couple of days before I had the courage to climb back on it again.

Arrangements were made for the last day of our stay to be set aside in order to attend a conducted tour to places of interest. Again the offer was made to us *pro gratis* by a local travel agency. One place we visited was the Natural Museum. The building itself was situated on the highest point of the town and from a vantage point nearby we captured a wonderful view of the natural phenomenon, known as the Three Sisters. It is a giant formation of rock rising from the depths of a vast gully and there mounted on the summit stood these rectangular figures which completely dominated mile upon mile of the dense forest surroundings. Nearby there was another tourist attraction, I think it was an old mine shaft, to get to the bottom we took a ride in a steel car or perhaps more accurately a bogie. Sitting four abreast each steel conveyor seated about twelve people. To secure the passengers a long steel bar which operated on a swivel was lowered across our midriffs. As the car moved off it proceeded along a flat plane into a dark cavern, the before I realised what was happening it seemed as though the car had tipped over the edge of a precipice as it plunged almost at right angles into the dark depths below. The experience was breathtaking.

Over the years I have returned to Katoomba three times and on each occasion I have always revisited the mine. Never once did it fail to scare the life out of me. Like it is said, all good things have to come to an end sometime, but for me it was all too soon. But not so for my old white nag, he didn't seem to mind at all. In fact he almost voiced his approval during the last day's trek. When I turned him round to head back to the stables for the last time, I couldn't hold the bugger back, it was the only gallop he produced all of the week.

On our journey back to Sydney we shared a compartment with a young Australian civilian, this was most unusual because most men of his age were overseas. He told us that he had been up north sheep-shearing. As I listened to his stories relating to the lives of such men I thought how lucky he was to have been born in a country that could offer so much adventure to young people. The only option open to me was to join one of the services. Having arrived back on board I was greeted with the news, up anchor. It was now time to say goodbye to all those parties and the generosity bestowed on us by the Australian people. Soon all submarines would be sailing north where no doubt many of us would be tempted to sample the delights of the Orient.

Shortly before the flotilla was due to leave Sydney I returned to the *Taurus* after all-night leave. As I passed through the control room my attention was drawn towards the activities of the outside tiffy, who having raised the periscope to what have should have been its maximum height seemed overwrought by its failure to do so. Anyone else would have walked passed and left him to it, but not me, I had to poke my nose in.

'What's the trouble?' I asked.

'I cannot get the cotter pin in place,' he answered.

This was a necessary precaution to enable a hand to be lowered into the well-hole to mop out any excessive amount of water which had dripped down from the periscope glands. My first reaction was to put my finger through the hole to see if I could feel the distance of the foul-up, this I thought was obviously caused by the malfunctioning of the hydraulic system. Suddenly without warning the impatient tiffy slammed down the operating lever leaving the tip of my finger inside the hole.

I then placed my bloody finger inches before his eyes and screamed out, 'Look what you have done, you scatty bastard.' Staring into his face I watched every drop of blood drain from it.

With his ashen cheeks, I thought that he was going to collapse and as he stood there trembling he said, 'You had better drink my tot.'

'No thanks, you need it more than I do,' I answered.

I then made a hasty report to the coxswain and made off to the North Shore Hospital.

On my arrival the doctor asked me, 'Have you got the other bit?'

'No it's still in the periscope,' I answered.

His only response was to instruct the nurse to give me what looked like a vaseline dressing. Anything short of an arm or a leg did not seem to bother him.

To alleviate the grief caused by nursing a sore finger for the next month, I was drafted to the parent ship *Adament* which was due to set sail for the Fiji Isle and because of my recent escapade with the three prisoners, life on board the *Taurus* held no future for me.

On board the *Adament* we lived in comparative luxury. At long last I was in the Navy that I meant to have joined many years before. We first dropped anchor off one of the remote Friendly Isles and we were told that we were the first man-o'-war to visit the island for twenty-five years. As the ship came to rest about half a mile off shore it seemed as if the whole island had sprung into life as hordes of natives piled into canoes which were hollowed out of huge trees. In minutes our ship was surrounded by brown-skinned natives some of whom were crowned with honey-coloured hair. As I gazed down from the upper deck I felt as though I had been hurled back two hundred years into the past.

That afternoon the captain allowed a party of them to

board the ship and wander round the mess-decks. When they came into the submarine spare-crew mess a few of us were playing darts. It was obvious that they had never seen anything like it in their lives before, they were fascinated with the game, so much so that we gave them a couple of sets of darts and a dartboard. To return the favour they did a war dance for us. The dance commenced when the party which numbered about twenty formed a circle in the middle of the mess-deck, while we in the spare crew gathered round them, their feet and body movements began at a slow pace in rhythm to the accompanying low chant of a native tongue. Gradually the pace of the dance increased with the faster rhythm and raised voices until they reached a peak when it appeared that they had spiked themselves into an uncontrollable frenzy, then suddenly they made as if to attack us with their crudely made weapons. As we sprang back to take cover our smiling faces gave way to looks of terror. Then to our relief the dance and the chanting gradually slowed down and the dance was ended.

Our next port of call was Suva, the capital of the Fiji Isles. While we were there I befriended a guy called Kemp. He was waiting to be discharged into civvy street.

'Before I take my time I want to have a tattoo put on my arm,' he said. After serving fourteen years without one I thought he was crazy. Most of the lads that I had joined up with, had one put on in the first week but I always resisted the temptation, mostly because of the expense. Right from my early days in the Navy I was indoctrinated with the philosophy that all money not spent on beer was wasted.

One day I was in one of the bars on the seafront when one of the locals pointed to a native and said, 'Look at his forehead and back, he is the only man in the world to have been inside the jaws of a killer shark and lived to tell the tale.' When I saw the extent of the scars I thought that his survival was surely a miracle.

We stayed in port about a week in which time AB Kemp was plastered from head to toe with every coloured tattoo imaginable. Although the tropical heat was causing a certain amount of discomfort to most of us he was quite prepared to suffer the soreness caused by the weeping needle holes. As for the tattooist as well as being a good artist he must have also dabbled in the science of hypnotism. How else could I account for such a sudden switch in the changed of personality by my new friend? At the time we were told the natives could walk barefooted through a pit of fire without harming themselves, if this was made possible by the inducement of hypnosis as we were told, it seemed likely that Kemp received the same treatment.

I never saw Kemp again after leaving Suva, that was because my life of luxury aboard the *Adament* came to an end when I was drafted to the submarine *Tally Ho*.

We had been at sea a few days when one of the seamen became critically ill with bowel trouble. In a turbulent sea which was worsening with each passing hour his condition had become an enormous responsibility for the captain to shoulder. In those days the nearest thing to a medic on board a submarine was a coxswain with a ball of cotton wool and a bottle of surgical spirit. In an effort to make him more comfortable the captain tried to help by forsaking his own bunk which being near amidships would be a little less subjected to the violent pitching in other parts of the boat. The nearest place where he could get medical care was Guadalcanal which had not long been recaptured from the Japs. It was not perhaps the ideal place to land him. From my own observations of the immediate surroundings I suspected that the best treatment that he could hope for would be administered from an army field hospital.

Looking back on those times now I am amazed how seldom such an emergency had been called for, we sometimes had things like boils and cuts which the coxswain had to deal with. I once did a three week patrol with a broken jaw which apparently mended with no treatment whatsoever.

It was during the forenoon when the *Tally Ho* came to rest alongside a temporary built jetty where the crew remained at harbour stations while the unfortunate seaman was carried by stretcher off the boat. Soon after when the crew had resumed to normal duties it was announced over the tannoy that one can of beer per man had been left on the casing by courtesy of the Yanks. Immediately we took to the ladders in a mad rush to sip the nectar of the gods. With can in hand we made for the gangway and as we did so, a giant-sized black soldier with the word 'Provost' written across the front of his helmet yelled out, 'Stay where you are, do not come ashore.'

Taking no notice whatsoever of his command we continued to surge forward while at the same time voicing our disapproval in very unfriendly terms. In an instant he levelled his service revolver straight at us.

'I mean business buddies,' he shouted.

It was only then we realised that it was no time to argue as we trampled over each other to get back on board. What strange people they are, these Yanks, first they give us beer then they want to shoot bloody great holes into us. Had we given any thought to the matter we would have realised that the ramshackle jetty was near to collapsing.

Within an hour we were once again heading in an northern direction towards Hong Kong where I was surprised to discover that piracy on the high seas was still prevalent in that part of the world. In fact the day before we arrived there, a pirate ship was audacious enough to enter Hong Kong Harbour where its crew boarded a ferry boat and robbed all of the passengers of their money and jewellery. Over the years I had heard many an old salt describing the luxurious standard of living an ordinary sailor could expect to enjoy on the China station and it was said that a stoker's meagre wage was ample to support a girlfriend and pay the rent on an uphomer's flat. In regards to the virtues of these young women, the old sea-dogs would readily spring to their defence when taunted by the gibes expressed by young rookies.

'What do they get up to when you put to sea?' they would ask. 'You have no worries about that, they are more faithful than some of the wives at home', they would jeer.

Needless to say none of that went down too well with the married men who had been separated from our wives for two years or more. However some of those romantic tales must have made some impression on me because I could not wait to get ashore to sample the goodies for myself. To my surprise trading was in full swing and we enjoyed a plentiful supply of food and drink. Bearing in mind that it was only a few weeks after Hong Kong had been freed from Japanese occupation I consider such diligence be a true testimony to the sound resilience which has so often been attributed to the Chinese people.

As the mountains surrounding Hong Kong Harbour dropped below the horizon the *Tally Ho* was once again at sea. This time we were set on a north-easterly course for Japan. For the likes of myself to set foot on the homeland of such strange people was an experience that in those days so very few sailors had the chance to enjoy. So with my mind crammed full of exotic fantasies I had every expectancy of an enjoyable time ahead. But all this was pie in the sky because when we arrived at Kure the first news that greeted us was that beer was almost non-existent. I said almost because each of us was given a chit which only allowed two cans of beer per man. To seasoned sailors' bellies that paltry amount would be about as satisfying as to feed a starving donkey with two strawberries. After a couple of days a few of us managed to get hold of some printed copies of the beer chits but we were faced with the problem of getting them franked with the ship's stamp, so we tried to transfer the various stamps in the back of our pay books by a licking and press method which I managed to get away with only once.

On my first run ashore I, along with two of my messmates, had a bit of luck when we wandered into a compound surrounded by a high wire-meshed fence. Its entrance was guarded by a Yankee sailor.

'Is there any chance of getting a can of beer around here?' I asked him.

'Sure,' he answered. 'Just open the door of that hut over there go in and drink as much as you want.'

We came across our first problem when we offered to pay for it in yen.

'That is no good to us,' they said.

'Well, what about sterling?' I asked.

'Give them a case full, I will pay for it,' cried out a benevolent Samaritan from the other side of the room, and so we spent the rest of the evening drinking for free with the Americans. After arriving back on board we discovered that we were the only ones in the crew to have found an oasis to quench our parched throats the snag was we made a mistake when we told them where the place was. I was watch aboard the following night, it was about midnight when the watch ashore began to drift back to the boat.

'Did you find the Yankee canteen?' I asked.

'Yes, but we got kicked out,' came the reply.

It was then left to my imagination what had happened. There are always those who would spoil a good thing. The next day I tried to restore Anglo-American relations with the sentry but sure enough my efforts got me no nearer than six yards from the entrance to the enclosure. The guy on sentry duty was no longer friendly towards me.

'After the ruckus last night all limeys are barred.'

'What happened then?' I asked. 'Your buddies thought that they could take over,' he drawled. So that put paid to all hopes of getting a drink that night. At the time we had received a month's payment in yen at the rate of forty-seven to the pound sterling. To distinguish them from those in circulation ashore, all notes were franked with the paymaster's stamp and were only meant to be spent in the canteen on board the parent ship. This was because the yen ashore was almost worthless. It soon became known that a small bag of sugar or a bar of chocolate had more bargaining power than a sack full of yen notes. Hence the elaborate rigging under the cover of bell-bottom trousers of all shore-going sailors. The odd wobbly sailor is not perhaps so unusual when returning from shore leave, but to see so many leaving the boat like it seemed rather strange.

From my viewpoint the area surrounding the dockside looked surprisingly absent of the massive devastation expected of an atomic bomb explosion but then again the large gaps between a few existing buildings suggested that a large clean-up operation had taken place. The stark reality of the situation did not hit me until a few days later. That was when two Yankee sailors offered a mess-mate and myself a lift into Hiroshima. Having no wish to reject the hand of friendship we climbed into the back of their jeep. Hardly had we time to get seated when the vehicle lunged forward with all the velocity of a launched space rocket.

As we raced towards the ruined city our driver and his co-operator were completely besotted in fits of wild hysteria as the two of us in the back clung to the shallow sides of the jeep so as to prevent our disintegrated bodies being lost in the midst of the clouds of grit and dust that trailed behind us. When we had travelled for some distance down what I imagined to have once been the main thoroughfare we were suddenly thrown forward with a sudden thrust as a result of our not so well meaning allies slamming on the brakes.

'This is as far as we go buddies,' and before we had time to come to our senses they had disappeared into thin air leaving us and the jeep by the roadside. As we scrambled to our feet we suddenly realised that our benevolent friends had procured the wheels without Uncle Sam's permission and we were left holding the baby. With the Yankee Provost guards just a few yards away it was time for us to scatter. By a stroke of luck we were nearby to one of the structures that still remained in one piece. We immediately took cover in what appeared to be an exclusive club for upmarket elderly male citizens none of whom opposed our sudden intrusion. We couldn't have wished for a better opportunity to unload our bars of chocolate and bags of sugar, and in no time at all they were bidding against each other. With our pockets stuffed full with yen notes we waved them goodbye with the feeling that we had done very well for ourselves.

Our only problem now was to get each note franked with the ship's stamp before we could buy goodies in the NAAFI. Soon after we had another stroke of luck. We had hardly walked a few yards down the road when we were beckoned into the house by half a dozen giggling geisha girls, once inside we were invited to get seated on a very low table where we experienced the age-old ritual of sipping lemon tea from very tiny cups. We were sitting there for a few minutes when one of the girls came to the table holding two Australian one pound notes and from the signs that she was making she indicated that she wanted me to change them for yen. Automatically hiding my enthusiasm I offered her the same rate as the Navy paymaster. This she gladly excepted and within a few minutes all her friends came running to the table all eager to dispose of their mouldies. We had only just settled the deal in the nick of time.

No sooner had we stuffed the notes into our pockets when two Yankee provos came barging into the room.

'You are off limits, get outside,' they bawled. Although both guys carried sidearms, the size of their huge frames was enough to discourage any opposition from such as I. Immediately I thought that they had linked us up with the stolen jeep, expecting to be arrested I was more than happy when they did not pursue the matter and left us to wander down the dirt road unheeded.

As we walked we were passing a never-ending queue of people many of whom were children suffering from terrible burns and goodness knows how many other complaints and diseases. While gazing into the expressionless faces of these poor souls the horror of war sickened me. Teams of medics operating from white tents which lined the roadside were unceasingly injecting limbs while others attended wounds of one kind or another. How many days or weeks this had been going on I do not know but after witnessing the plight of these people I was somehow relieved of all the bitterness that I had felt towards them. Further down to our left other streets were barricaded off with long poles each of them bearing do not enter signs – typhoid, cholera, and all kinds of diseases. Looking back after all these years I ask myself for what reason we submariners were subjected to such a lethal environment. Was it curiosity, ignorance, or were we used as guinea pigs to test the rate of survival? After a few days we moved round to Nagasaki where I was to witness scenes identical to those in Hiroshima. If anything it was even more horrendous. There were no tears to be shed when the boat was ordered to proceed to Singapore, and as for the eastern promise none of it materialised. Almost as soon as we arrived there we received the long-awaited signal. The boat with its crew was recalled to the UK.

Chapter Twelve

Homeward Bound

We stayed in port just long enough to store ship and take on fuel and water, then at last we were bound for the UK. Now that hostilities had ceased the whole voyage would be made on the surface, any discomfort caused by being tossed about would be well compensated for when getting the opportunity to fill our lungs with fresh air. The anguish of being attacked by hostile aircraft or enemy submarines no longer troubled us so we were having a very enjoyable time while crossing the Indian Ocean. It was a real luxury for us members of the engine room branch to be allowed on the bridge to take a breath of fresh air, that was a pleasure that we were never allowed to enjoy in wartime.

The Oerlikon gun was mounted on a platform behind the bridge. Now since the gun was no longer required and the platform was devoid of all personnel, I asked the officer of the watch if I could sling my hammock across the guard rail.

'I don't see why not,' was his reply.

Within a few minutes I had taken full advantage of my successful request. There I was settled down under the tropical stars being charmed into a peaceful sleep by the sound of the monotonous drone of the engine exhaust as it pounded the inner walls of the muffler tank. I must confess that I know very little about seamanship but I would take an educated guess that the officer of the watch became quite envious of the sleeping beauty when suddenly he ordered the helm watchkeeper to turn the wheel hard a starboard. That was when I awoke with a shock when suddenly a full sea hit me broadside on, swamping the gun platform and filling my hammock to the brim. Cursing and swearing I leapt on to the iron deck and quickly untied my saturated bedding, in a mad rush to dry myself out in the hot engine room below. Meanwhile the whole watch on the bridge was creased up in hysterics.

'That will teach you,' someone shouted as I made haste through the conning tower hatch.

My thoughts now turned to home and realising that my son would be going into his fourth year. I remembered myself at that age. One of the greatest thrills of my childhood days was when my grandfather built me a fort which he garrisoned with numerous coloured toy soldiers which were armoured with cannons. During the harsh years that followed the First World War, such a prize possession was something to be envied by any child. With these thoughts in mind I set about building one for my son. Having all the necessary components in a well stocked store entirely at my disposal, I was well equipped to take on the task which would occupy every moment of my spare time until I arrived at Port Said.

The first thing that came into my possession was a plywood box which, when turned upside down, was the ideal size to form a rampart on which to mount the towers. I remembered being told that my grandfather had toiled for many hours doing a tedious job gluing pieces of cardboard together when making the towers. I can also remember his dismay when he discovered that I had completely wrecked it in less than half the time it took him to build it.

So I decided to build my son's towers out of tin and solder, both of which were in plentiful supply in the store. To decorate it with a rock-like finish I would first varnish it and while it was still wet, sprinkle it with sand. My only problem was, How could I get hold of sand in the middle of the ocean? Save for the painting, the fort was completed by the time we had reached the Bitter Lakes which is about halfway through the Suez Canal.

It was daytime when an enterprising Arab had paddled his boat from a distance of well over a mile to find out if he could trade with us. That was my chance to get the sand. After a laborious time making all sorts of hand signs and miming gestures, I managed to convey to him that I wanted some sand. To my surprise he was quite willing to head for the shore only to return with half the Sahara desert packed into a bloody great sack. When I tossed a few coins into his boat he promptly responded to my generosity by throwing his arms into the air while ranting and raging like a demented lunatic. Then to add salt to his wounds he couldn't believe his eyes when I tipped nearly all of the sand over the side. I only wanted a handful to do the job.

After his overnight stay ashore, the official pilot took up his position on the bridge and once again we were under way and heading towards Port Said where he would be discharged from his duties as navigator aboard the *Tally Ho*. By then most of us in the boat were ready to down a few beers but first I had some shopping to do. Thinking that toy soldiers would be more obtainable in Port Said than they would be at home I spent all the daylight hours searching the shops and markets. The only ones that I could find were crudely made flat solid lead figures with practically no colouring at all and bore little resemblance to what I remembered as a boy. Anyway they would have to suffice until something better came my way.

With my shopping completed it was time for a few beers, it was just beginning to get dark when I wandered into one of the larger bars on the main street. Inside facing the entrance was a large dance floor surrounded by tables and chairs with all drinks being supplied by waiter service only. I sat at the table just inside by the entrance door. Facing me at the far end of the hall a dance band was playing the modern dance tunes of that time. The stage from which they were playing was perched high up in the air with a flight of stairs at either end. For a while everybody seemed to be enjoying the music while sipping their beer in a blissful mood. As the evening wore on, hordes of rowdy soldiers wearing chindit hats poured into the hall. Suddenly all havoc broke loose when half a dozen of them climbed on to the stage and set about ejecting all of the bandsmen from their seats and seizing their instruments. With such an unruly mob at large the few waiters had no chance of controlling the situation, one of them did manage to fight his way into the street where he shouted out for help. Within seconds a lone red-cap came racing towards the stage. He was about halfway there, when a soldier put his foot out sending him crashing to the floor. Before being knocked unconscious by soldiers wielding chairs on him, he managed to blow a whistle. When his colleague came rushing in to help, he got exactly the same treatment, as he lay almost unconscious on the floor he reached for his pistol and fired a shot into the crowd that were now rushing to get out of the building.

As I sat glued to my chair in shock, a tough-looking guy dragged me towards the street.

'This is no time to hang about here,' he shouted.

Out on the pavement I was horrified to see one of the soldiers in a state of collapse being helped by his friends. Having paused for a moment to look, I was once again jostled along the street by someone who was much too big for me to argue with. When I returned to the boat the following morning a colleague on another submarine nearby to where the *Tally Ho* was berthed, noticed my growth of whiskers.

'I wouldn't go ashore if I were you, they are looking for a bearded matelot,' he shouted over to me.

The boat was leaving for home the next morning so there was no way that I was going to risk staying behind as a witness in a Court Martial, so I made no attempt to probe into the authenticity of his statement As expected we sailed for Malta the next day. The thousand mile trip would only take a few days so I was looking forward to renewing some of my old acquaintances ashore. I hoped that the people on the island would have by that time recovered from the siege. But I was disappointed to find that it was not so. Almost every building that surrounded the harbour had been demolished. The devastation was so vast that the whole place was unrecognisable. The people on the island still on the verge of starvation could hardly find enough food to feed themselves so there was no chance of us feasting on Charlie's Big Eats down the Gut. We were only to pleased to leave it all behind us when starting out on the next leg of our journey.

Before leaving, news had reached the mess that two or three officers had joined the boat to take passage home. From which of the services they belonged I am not sure, but the buzz was that they were being lavishly entertained by the captain who went completely off his rocker during the time we were in Gibraltar. Through his dogmatic attitude towards his subordinates, he showed utter contempt as regards their feelings. Contrary to the captain's robust build, the first lieutenant was a much smaller man who seemingly took no part in trying to curtail the captain's wild antics. I think it was our last night in Gibraltar when his strange behaviour reached its climax. It was very late in the evening when those of us on board were suddenly awakened by the continues clanging of the motor room telegraph gongs and the thrashing of the screws which were directly below our mess deck. I leapt from my bunk and ran into the motor room and to my horror I saw the two strange officers who were taking passage operating the main switches without any supervision whatsoever. They seemed completely oblivious of the danger.

I then rushed into the control room and when reaching the conning tower ladder, I looked up into the darkness shouting, 'What the bloody hell's going on up there?' No sooner had the words left my lips when one of the large light bulbs exploded as it hit the iron rungs of the ladder and leaving the splintered glass all about my face and head.

'Who the hell's up there?' I asked a bystander.

'The Captain,' he answered.

All the time this was going on the boat still remained tied up to the destroyer which by this time must have been dragged towards the rocks. I don't know who it was that eventually came to their senses and called the duty watch to harbour stations, but I do remember that it was well into the night before all was secure again. The following night when we were leaving harbour there was once again one hell of a racket coming from the bridge, and with the boat's siren screaming out, everyone in Gibraltar would have been alerted.

Much to everyone's relief the remaining part of the voyage home continued without further incidents. When we finally berthed in our home port we were still closed up at harbour stations when the buzz spread through the boat that an escort party was waiting on the quay ready to take the captain back to Gibraltar for a court martial. One of my mess-mates was also summoned to attend as a witness. They called on him because at the time he was employed doing quartermaster's duties. It was some weeks before I saw my friend again and the only statement that he made about the case was that while he was waiting outside the court martial room to be called upon to give evidence, the captain was marched through.

As he passed my friend he turned to him saying, 'Forget your loyalties and just tell the truth.'

I remained on the boat for a while, at the time there were disputes going on between the electrical unions and the employees' bosses. Because of the strikes that followed, submarines were directed to different localities to supply emergency electricity for the different dockyards. I was more than pleased when the *Tally Ho* was sent to Chatham. For me it meant that for two nights out of three I could go home.

When the workers' dispute was finally brought to a settlement so ended my nightly visits home. The *Tally Ho* was recalled to Dolphin where she joined up with the half a dozen 'T' class submarines which were in the reserve group. In the meantime the *Thermopylae* had just completed a refit and was fitted out with a snortmast, being the first of our submarines to be equipped with one. I had the honour of operating it throughout the three months trials. With the two main engines greedily hogging a limited air supply meant that for all that time we were living in a partial vacuum. Such conditions led to the rumour that we would all be made sterile. It was sometime after my next leave before I could prove this wild statement to be a load of hooey.

Finally the day came when I was put on draft to Dolphin ready for my discharge into civvy street. That morning I must to have had dozens of sippers and gulpers from all my crew-mates because I almost had to be carried to the quarterdeck of the *Montclare* which was our parent ship. Somehow I managed to find my way down the gangway and into the motorboat. As it turned to take me ashore I think the whole crew had turned out to wave me farewell, as I turned to take a last look at the *Montclare* I could see them all waving and shouting.

Their last parting words rang out across the Clyde,

'You'll be back.'

I could hear it being repeated over and over again. It was well into the evening the following day before I stepped from the pinnace on to the pier at Fort Blockhouse. Up to that time I had given no thought as to how I would acquire a full kitbag, as for replacing my kit after it was lost on the *Medway* other options had taken priority. I only owned one shore-going suit, a shift of underwear and a pair of overalls.

Later that evening when I went to investigate the contents of my kit bag I could not believe what my old crewmates had done. When I turned the bag upside down to empty it, all the *Montclare*'s mess-traps rattled and crashed on to the deck in Platypus hut. There were mess fannies, dinner plates, cups, saucers, knives and forks, and goodness knows what else they had stuffed into it.

When I got paid my war gratuities on the following day I was informed that because of an offence that I had committed four months before the war started, I would not get paid the first year's gratuity, which was the enormous sum of twenty-five pounds. That for me was the last straw, there was no way that I was going to sign on for another ten after that. With just a few days in which to serve I was recalled to Chatham which was my original port division. As I walked through Pembroke's main gates I wondered if the regulating staff had relented with regard to their orders that all submariners should not wear the submarine cap ribbon while they were in Pembroke barracks. It was on a previous occasion during my stay there they tried to stop us from wearing them, we kicked up such a stink about it that in the end they had to surrender to us obstinate proud wearers.

Out of twenty-five of us trainees who joined up together there were only four of us left. All the others had found watery graves. The war had taken a heavy toll on the lives of Whacker's 1937 first trainees.

During the morning of our last day in the Navy we had

to return our gas mask and hammock to their appropriate departments, but as usual I had no hammock to hand in because someone had the cheek to nick the one that I had acquired. Anyhow the old three badge supply killick in the store room found a way to solve the problem. He said to go and see his chum in the next hut who could sell me an old hammock cheaply. After a big row, to save time I was compelled to heed his advice. But when I saw the bloody thing that I paid good money for I could have almost cried, the canvas hammock had been used so much it had holes in it. With the proceeds of the racket the pair of them must have made enough money to buy a Navy of their own.

The fleet reserve office was to be our last call. Although my three chums were persuaded to sign on the dotted line, I told the chief that I wanted no part of it.

'You will get paid for it,' he said. 'There will not be another war in our lifetime.'

How wrong he was. When only a few months had passed I bought a morning paper. There they were all three of them pictured on the front page. 'Off to Korea', the caption read.

With all routine completed the four of us made our way to the main gates where we caught a bus to the town centre, where we split up. Two of us went headlong towards the Red Lion. After three hours soaking up rum chasers we staggered out to the pavement then throwing our hats in the air we were screaming out, 'No more Navy!'

Soon a huge audience had gathered to watch our antics, everybody seemed to be enjoying the fun until two Navy patrolmen pounced on me and threw me into a nearby van and my pal got the same treatment.

'You can't touch us,' I shouted, 'we have been discharged.'

'Oh yes, we can,' said the crusher who appeared from nowhere.

After questioning us, his mood changed. 'I am going to be lenient with you two, I am taking you to the station and putting you on a train. You can do what you like outside of Chatham but if I see you back here you will be put inside for three months.'